BERKHAMSTED

A HISTORY & CELEBRATION

THE BERKHAMSTED LOCAL HISTORY AND MUSEUM SOCIETY

THE FRANCIS FRITH COLLECTION

www.francisfrith.co.uk

First published in the United Kingdom in 2005
by The Francis Frith Collection®

Hardback Edition 2005
ISBN 1-84589-195-3

British Library Cataloguing in Publication Data

Berkhamsted - A History & Celebration
The Berkhamsted Local History and Museum Society

The Francis Frith Collection
Frith's Barn, Teffont,
Salisbury, Wiltshire SP3 5QP
Tel: +44 (0) 1722 716 376
Email: info@francisfrith.co.uk
www.francisfrith.co.uk

Printed and bound in England

Front Cover: **BERKHAMSTED, TOWN HALL c1910** ZZZ04935t
(Berkhamsted Local History and Museum Society)

Additional modern photographs by Ken Wallis unless otherwise specified.

Domesday extract used in timeline by kind permission of
Alecto Historical Editions, www.domesdaybook.org
Aerial photographs reproduced under licence from
Simmons Aerofilms Limited.
Historical Ordnance Survey maps reproduced under licence from
Homecheck.co.uk

Every attempt has been made to contact copyright holders of illustrative material. We will be happy to give full acknowledgement in future editions for any items not credited. Any information should be directed to The Francis Frith Collection.

The colour-tinting in this book is for illustrative purposes only, and is not intended to be historically accurate

AS WITH ANY HISTORICAL DATABASE, THE FRANCIS FRITH ARCHIVE IS CONSTANTLY BEING CORRECTED AND IMPROVED, AND THE PUBLISHERS WOULD WELCOME INFORMATION ON OMISSIONS OR INACCURACIES

CONTENTS

BERKHAMSTED FROM THE AIR 1960 AFA79898

c500 BC Grim's Ditch, Woodcock Hill, constructed

AD60 Northchurch Roman villa in occupation

c800 Saxon church at Northchurch

970 First mention of Berkhamsted in will of Lady Elgiva

Roman Britain | **Dark Ages**

49BC Julius Caesar crosses the Rubicon

AD79 Eruption of Vesuvius destroying Pompeii

AD122 Emperor Hadrian orders Hadrian's Wall to be built

AD455 Vandals sack Rome

AD520 Possible period of King Arthur legend

AD871 King Alfred and Danelaw

1541 Berkhamsted School founded by John Incent, Dean of St Paul's

1580 Elizabeth I leases Manor of Berkhamsted to Sir Edward Carey

1618 James I grants Charter of Incorporation. Berkhamsted becomes free borough

1620 First 'Battle of Berkhamsted Common'

1684 John Sayer, chief cook to Charles II, provides almshouses

Tudor Period | **Stuart Britain**

1509 Henry VIII becomes king

1558 Accession of Elizabeth 1

1588 Spanish Armada defeated

1600 Founding of East India Company

1605 Gunpowder Plot

1649 Charles I executed

1666 Great Fire of London

1688-89 Glorious Revolution

1837 Railway reaches Berkhamsted

c1840 Arrival of William Cooper, inventor of sheep dip

1859 Town Hall and Market House built

1866 Second 'Battle of Berkhamsted Common'

1888 Berkhamsted Girls' Grammar School founded

1900 Lower Mill ceases operation

Victorian Britain | **Edwardian Era**

1837 Victoria becomes queen

1846 Repeal of Corn Laws

1851 Great Exhibition at Crystal Palace

1885 Karl Benz designs first automobile

1899-1902 Boer War

1901 Queen Victoria dies

1903 Campaign for women's suffrage begins

1910 Edward VII dies

HISTORICAL TIMELINE FOR BERKHAMSTED

Middle Ages

1066 William of Normandy offered crown of England at Berkhamsted

1066 Battle of Hastings. Norman rule begins

1086 Berkhamsted features in Domesday Book

1086 Domesday Book

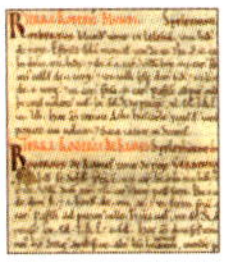

1156 Henry II's charter confirms rights of citizens dating from Saxon times

1170 Murder of Thomas à Becket at Canterbury cathedral

1215 Magna Carta

1222 St Peter's Church consecrated

1306 Robert the Bruce declares himself King of Scotland

Late Medieval

1348 Black Death kills 25 million in Europe

1361 The Black Prince honeymoons at the castle

1415 Battle of Agincourt

1485 Battle of Bosworth Field marks end of Plantaganet dynasty

1495 Cicely, Duchess of York, dies in the castle

Georgian Era

1731 William Cowper born in Rectory

1737 Thomas Bourne's Charity School opens

1739 John Wesley founds Methodist church

1762 Mozart performs at the age of 6

1789 French Revolution

1798 Grand Junction Canal opens as far as Tring

1815 Battle of Waterloo

1825 Stockton to Darlington Railway

20th Century Britain

1914 First World War begins

1914-18 Inns of Court OTC based in Berkhamsted

1926 John Logie Baird obtains first television picture

1935 Foundling Hospital moves to Berkhamsted

1938 Rex Cinema built, designed by David Nye

1939 Outbreak of Second World War

1956 Suez Crisis

1965 Electrification of railway

1966 England win World Cup

1969 First man on the Moon

1974 Local Government reorganisation

1982 Falklands Conflict

1997 Closure of former Cooper works

2004 Rex Cinema re-opens

CHAPTER ONE

A HOMESTEAD AMONG THE BIRCHES

SITUATED a mere 30 miles north-west of London, Berkhamsted is a linear town set in the fertile valley of the Bulbourne. Now little more than a stream, this river once flowed strongly enough to power at least two mills, the Upper and the Lower Mills, both mentioned in Domesday. The modern High Street follows much the same route as the ancient Roman road, Akeman Street, an important trade route through the Chilterns. The area was thickly wooded, as the meaning of the Saxon name denotes, 'homestead among birches', and trees are still very much a feature of Berkhamsted's landscape. South of the High Street, roads with houses rise steeply from the valley bottom. On the other side, where there were once water meadows, the valley broadens out, making room for the canal and the railway; beyond is the Norman castle, the site of so many important events. Behind this, roads of later housing climb up the hill to the Common and the open countryside beyond.

From the earliest times people have been drawn to Berkhamsted, firstly because of its strategic position and good connections to London and the Midlands (whether by road, canal, or rail), secondly because of its favourable climate, and thirdly because of its attractive position. They have for the most part stayed because it is a pleasant place in which to live, with a thriving, vibrant community. It is the people of Berkhamsted who have made the town what it is today; hundreds of people, many very ordinary, who at different times have shown their independent spirit and fought for their rights, or have recognised the politically expedient moment to take action. It is thanks to those people that we have a Norman castle in Berkhamsted, that the Common remains as the largest common in the south of England, that we can enjoy the beauty of the Ashridge Estate, that the Town Hall still stands today, and that the Rex Cinema recently reopened - and there is much more besides. Come with

THE CASTLE c1960 B407050

New housing has since spread the town further up the hillside, but the skyline remains unspoilt.

us on our journey through time; walk along Berkhamsted's streets, and meet some of those people who have helped to mould the town we know today.

It is likely that the valley of the Bulbourne was settled from the earliest times by people using the local resources of timber, clay, flints and iron ore. Although prehistoric finds are rare, a number of Neolithic date have been found on both sides of the valley. When the A41 bypass was built in the 1990s, Neolithic and Bronze Age flints and roundhouses of the late Bronze Age were found near Oakwood. On the south-west edge of the town, near Egerton-Rothesay School, there is an interesting bank and ditch earthwork, known as Grim's Ditch. It was probably constructed during the late Bronze Age, perhaps as a territorial boundary.

In the late Iron Age the valley appears to have been a major iron production centre. Its strategic value as a route through the Chilterns made it ideal for exploiting this demand for iron. Four 1st-century shaft furnaces were found when Bridgewater Middle School was being built in the 1970s, close to four late Iron Age cremation burials, ditches, and pits of similar date. The Berkhamsted Common Grim's Ditch is a much larger structure than that on the south side of the valley, and appears to be a late Iron Age or early Roman cross-ridge dyke, controlling a large area. Late Iron Age coins have been found in different areas of the town. During the early Roman period iron production appears to have declined, and had probably ceased altogether by the end of the Roman period.

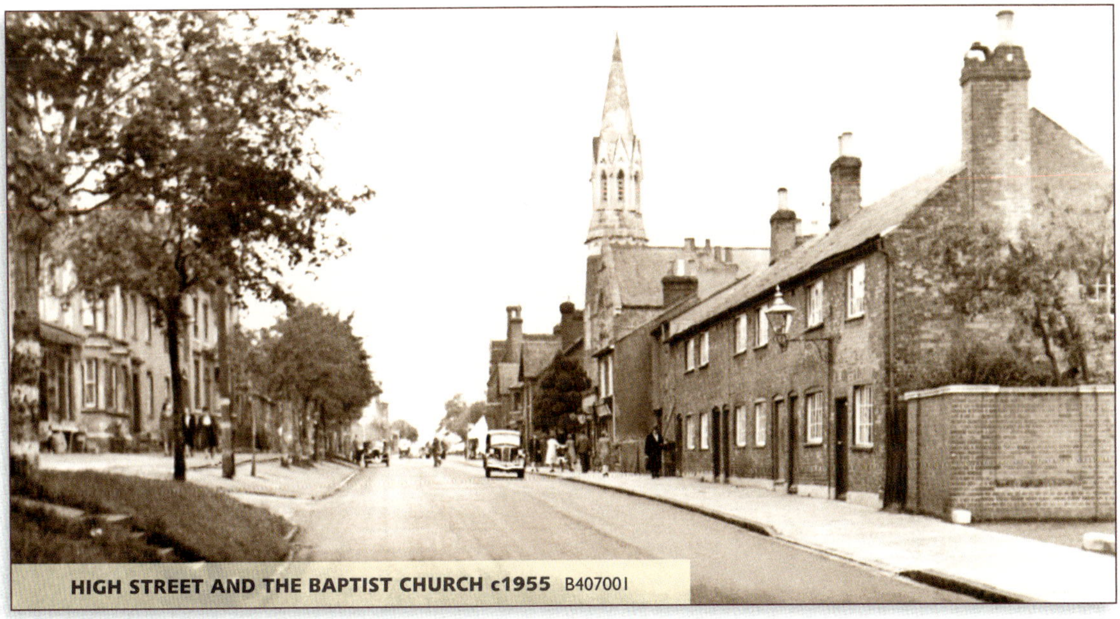

HIGH STREET AND THE BAPTIST CHURCH c1955 B407001

This view looks towards the town centre from the east; this scene remains much the same today.

Fact File

One of the best-known traders in the early 19th century dealt in ironwork. James Wood produced a range of ironware, including candle-snuffers, rat-traps, skewers, meat safes, fireguards, and sieves. The firm still trades in the town today, but now focuses on a nursery and giftware business.

Roman finds in Berkhamsted are concentrated along Akeman Street, and evidence shows roadside occupation. Pottery, building materials and iron were found at 142 High Street, Northchurch. Other finds, including the possible construction layer of the highway, are recorded near St John's Well Lane, close to the sorting office. A Roman lamp was found at the former gas works in Billet Lane. These suggest extensive but scattered occupation north of the High Street. North of Berkhamsted Castle, two flint and tile walls of a substantial building were discovered in 1970, suggesting that the building of the castle damaged part of a Roman building. Small-scale excavations at the edge of the golf course in 1954 revealed

UPPER MILL c1880 ZZZ04917 (Berkhamsted Local History and Museum Society)

The mill was demolished in 1927 to make room for the Music School of Berkhamsted School (now the Collegiate School).

masonry foundations and tesserae, but little is known of the structure. A substantial villa was found close to the river in 1973 during housing development in Northchurch.

Until recently the only known remains of Saxon Berkhamsted were the south and west walls of Berkhamsted St Mary's, referred to since the 14th century as Northchurch. Possibly this Saxon church was built by the lords of a large estate, which became the medieval manor of Berkhamsted, but no trace of this has been found. The Saxon church would have been a small two-cell structure and built of flint. Two recent finds add to our knowledge of Saxon Berkhamsted. In 1999, pottery, including several early to mid Saxon sherds and many more Saxo-Norman sherds, were found at Incents Lawn, Chesham Road, not far from the High Street. In the same year more pottery of the same period, AD 1000-1150, was found on the site of the Cooper sheep-dip works. It is likely also that the two mills date from the late 9th century. Reference to the name Berkhamsted first appears in a document dated AD 970, the will of the Lady Elgiva.

We do not know whether the Saxon town of Berkhamsted was in Northchurch or further east nearer the present town centre. Immediately before the Norman Conquest, Edmar, a thane under Earl Harold, was encamped at Berkhamsted, from where he ruled the local area. In 1066 an event took place in Berkhamsted which was to change the course of English history. After the defeat of Harold at the battle of Hastings on 14 October 1066, Duke William of Normandy marched with his army through southern England, pillaging as he went. Crossing the Thames at Wallingford, he reached Berkhamsted. Here he was met by Archbishop Ealdred, the Bishops of Worcester and Hereford, Earls Eadwin and Morcar, and the chief men of London, who swore allegiance to him, and offered him the crown. Continuing to pillage as he went, William proceeded to London, where he was crowned king on Christmas Day 1066.

BERKHAMSTED ST MARY'S

In the 13th century a more elaborate cruciform church was created from the original Saxon church when the present chancel and transepts were built. The present tower was built in the 15th century. In 1881 one of the Saxon walls was removed in order to add the north aisle. At the same time, vestries were built on the north side of the chancel and the south porch was added. There are a number of interesting relics and monuments to many notable people of Northchurch. The Prince of Wales is Patron to the living of Berkhamsted St Mary.

THE BAYEUX TAPESTRY

The Bayeux Tapestry depicts the Norman Conquest of England. It is usually attributed to William's wife, Matilda, but it was more likely commissioned by William's half-brother, Bishop Odo of Bayeux, for display in Bayeux Cathedral. From its style, it is thought to have been embroidered in England. It is incomplete. Two missing panels at the end are believed to have portrayed the Saxons' submission at Berkhamsted and William on the throne of England. These panels were reconstructed by Jan Messent in 1997 for Madeira Threads (UK) Ltd. The Latin inscription means: 'And here at Berkhamsted (Beorcham), the nobles of London submit. Archbishop Ealdred. Here sits William, King of the English. All rejoice.' These panels were displayed at a special exhibition in the town in 1998.

THE BAYEUX TAPESTRY RECONSTRUCTION 1997 ZZZ04898 (Reproduced by kind permission of Jan Messent)

William granted the Manor and Honour of Berkhamsted to his half-brother Robert, Count of Mortain. Berkhamsted was of strategic importance, since there was already a Saxon fort guarding the main route north through the valley. Robert set about building a strongly fortified castle, a typical Norman motte and bailey castle, with a tower or keep built on an earthen mound surrounded by a defensive enclosure. The castle was constructed at the bottom of a dry valley where there were springs to fill the moats. This first castle was a timber structure. Even in its ruined state, the castle remains the best example of a motte and bailey castle in the country, in fact a unique example, since it has two moats and in some places even three! We do not know whether Robert built his castle on the site of the Saxon fortification or whether that structure had been at the top of present-day Castle Hill.

We hear of Berkhamsted next in the Domesday Book, 1086. The entry shows 37 households. An interesting feature is the large vineyard. There was also a priest. Within the manor was the borough with 12 burgesses (the figure 52 is probably a copyist's mistake) and two watermills. We do not know whether the borough recorded here was a Norman foundation, or whether it had existed in the late Saxon period. It is possible that it was regarded as a borough by ancient right, since a royal charter granted in 1156 by Henry II confirmed privileges enjoyed by the citizens since the time of the Saxon king, Edward the Confessor.

THE OLD MILL, SITE OF THE LOWER MILL 2005 ZZZ04944 (Ken Wallis)

This mill closed in 1900 because of insufficient water in the river. The great iron water wheel remained until it was removed for salvage in the Second World War.

THE DOMESDAY ENTRY

'The land of the Count of Mortain. In Tring Hundred. The Count of Mortain holds Berchehastede. It answers for 13 hides. Land for 26 ploughs. In lordship 6 hides; 3 ploughs, another 3 possible. A priest with 14 villeins and 15 smallholders have 12 ploughs, another 8 possible. There, 6 serfs, and a certain ditcher has half a hide, and Rannulf, a serving-man of the Count, 1 virgate. In the borough of this town, 52 burgesses who render £4 from toll, and they have half a hide. 2 mills yielding 20s. 2 arpents of vines. Meadow for 8 ploughs. Pasture for the livestock of the vill. Woodland for 1,000 swine and 5s too. In all it is worth £16. When he received it, £20. In the time of King Edward, £24. Edmar, a thegn of Earl Harold, held this manor.'

Fact File

Until very recently, Peter Latchford produced Frithsden wines from his vineyard in the nearby village of Frithsden. Furthermore, on the southern slopes of the town, on the Sunnyside Allotments, vines are still grown today, as we can see in the photograph, below.

GRAPE VINES, SUNNYSIDE ALLOTMENTS 2005
ZZZ04945 (Ken Wallis)

Berkhamstedians may exaggerate the importance of Berkhamsted Castle in national history, but no one can deny that much of the town's early history would be lacking if the castle had never existed. It brought extra trade to Berkhamsted, making it a good market town at an early date. The castle's links with royalty (and here the proximity of the royal palace at Kings Langley played a part) probably influenced the granting of some of the early charters. Geoffrey Fitz Piers, Earl of Essex, one of the occupants of the castle, was instrumental in building St Peter's Church. Another occupant, Edmund, Earl of Cornwall, founded the monastery at Ashridge.

The oldest flint and stonework of the castle ruins date from the mid 12th century, the time when Thomas à Becket was Lord Chancellor. The stone would have come from Totternhoe, near Dunstable, where a lime and stone works still exists today. The castle was well defended, with two moats and three sets of earthworks around an oblong bailey, and a further moat around the motte. The substantial motte stands at the north-east corner, commanding views over the present town and surrounding countryside. On the top are the foundations of the circular keep, 18m in diameter, within which is a well. The flint rubble core of the curtain wall survives for almost the entire circuit of the bailey. The outer defences have also survived, apart from the damage caused by the building of the railway in 1837, and by the road immediately to the west in the 1930s. Access to the castle is now from the south-west, but the castle's main entrance was to the south, at the end of Castle Street, and would have been from a wooden drawbridge across the moat.

Space does not allow a full history of the castle to the end of the 15th century, when it fell into decay. We can only highlight the main points of interest. At the death of William the Conqueror in 1087 the succession of his son, William Rufus, was disputed, among others, by Robert Mortain, who was consequently dispossessed of Berkhamsted. Later, re-instated, he was one of the few nobles to remain loyal at Henry I's accession. However, his son, William Mortain, was later in dispute with Henry I; he was dispossessed and ended his life in captivity.

It is unclear what happened to Berkhamsted Castle during the complicated history of Stephen's reign (1135-54), but during the reigns of Henry I and Henry II, the castle was in the hands of chancellors, first Randulph and later Thomas à Becket. We know that in 1123 Henry I held court here, and that in 1156 Henry II granted a royal charter to the merchants of Berkhamsted. This confirmed the laws and customs enjoyed under Edward the Confessor, William I and Henry I, and freed them from all tolls and dues. This charter also decreed that no market could be set up within seven miles of the town. During the time of Thomas à Becket (1155-1164), entries in the Pipe Rolls indicate extensive building works.

Richard I began the royal tendency of disregarding the castle when he gave it to his queen, Berengaria, in 1191. She lived here until Richard's death in 1199. In 1204 King John granted the Honour to his queen, Isabella, who remained in residence until 1216. The building works under Thomas à Becket had supposedly made the castle impregnable, but when it was besieged by Prince Louis of France in 1216, it held out for only two weeks.

In 1227 Richard, Earl of Cornwall, younger brother of Henry III, was granted the castle. He made it one of his main residences; in 1254 he built a tower of three storeys, and in 1269 he carried out extensive repairs to the barbican, the keep and turrets, and various royal chambers.

Fact File

The coat of arms of Richard, Earl of Cornwall, with 13 gold balls is incorporated in Berkhamsted's coat of arms; it can be seen on the wooden post in the High Street outside the Civic Centre, and also on the front of the former Bourne Charity School, founded in 1731 and extended in 1853, now the Britannia Building Society.

In 1270 Richard and his son, Edmund, who had been born at the castle, brought back from Germany a phial said to contain some of the blood of Christ. On succeeding to the earldom, Edmund presented part of the blood to Hailes Abbey. The remainder he kept until 1276, when he founded a religious house at Ashridge and installed a small order of monks, the Bonhommes, to manage it. Edward I held a parliament at Ashridge in 1291. Later, in 1376, the monastery was richly endowed by the Black Prince.

THE MONKS' GARDEN, ASHRIDGE COLLEGE, BERKHAMSTED c1960 B407066

A peaceful reminder of Ashridge's foundation as a College of the Bonhommes, these gardens have since been renovated.

Edward I granted Berkhamsted to his second queen, Margaret of France. On her death, Isabella, queen of Edward II, succeeded to the Manor. In 1337 Edward III gave the castle to his son Edward, the Black Prince, as part of the newly created Duchy of Cornwall. The castle is still part of the Duchy of Cornwall's estate today.

King John of France was imprisoned here after the battle of Poitiers in 1356. In 1361 the Black Prince married Joan, the Fair Maid of Kent, and they honeymooned in Berkhamsted. The castle had an extensive deer park, which was a favourite hunting ground for the prince. A brass commemorating John Raven, squire to the Black Prince, can be seen in St Peter's Church; he is remembered in the road name Raven's Lane to this day.

Fact File

When the Black Prince left Berkhamsted to fight at the battles of Poitiers and Crécy he took with him archers from Berkhamsted and nearby, including Stephen of Champneys, Edward le Bourne, Richard of Gaddesden, and Henry of Berkhamsted. Berkhamsted archers practised shooting in 'butts' near the centre of the town on what is now called Butts Meadow.

JOHN RAVEN'S BRASS, ST PETER'S CHURCH
ZZZ04899 (Berkhamsted Local History and Museum Society)

BERKHAMSTED PARK

In medieval times, parks were places where deer were kept for hunting and the raising of venison. Parks were also used to produce timber and for grazing other livestock. They were 'wood pastures', remnants of earlier 'wastes', enclosed and preserved for manorial lords. Berkhamsted Park was probably created in the 12th century. The earliest reference is in 1302, when 'William called Hereford of Berchampstede' was given the 'custody for life of the wood of Berchampstede and the Park and Warren'. He received 5½d a day, a robe worth ten shillings, and 'all the wood blown down in that wood and Park and the trunks of the trees thrown down there.' He was responsible for looking after the deer and guarding them from poachers. Through the centuries there are references to the erection of pales to contain the deer and to enlargements through enclosures. A map of the 'Honour of Berkhamsted and Terrier or Particulars of Castle, Demesne and Waste Land', made in 1849, shows the park covering an area of some 1,000 acres, and well timbered. Berkhamsted Park remained in existence until the 1960s, when new housing was built on its south-facing slopes up to the trees on the skyline.

CHARLES H ASHDOWN'S IMPRESSION OF THE CASTLE AND PALACE OF BERKHAMPSTEAD IN THE TIME OF EDWARD IV ZZZ04900 (Berkhamsted Local History and Museum Society)

In 1389 Geoffrey Chaucer was appointed Clerk of the Works at Berkhamsted Castle and other royal properties. It is not known how much time he spent in Berkhamsted, but he is known to have been a friend of John of Gaddesden, who lived in nearby Little Gaddesden, the model for his Doctor of Phisick in 'The Canterbury Tales'.

On his accession in 1399, Henry IV granted the castle and estates to his son and heir, later King Henry V, from whom it then passed to Margaret of Anjou, queen to Henry VI. In 1469 Edward IV granted Berkhamsted to his mother, Cicely, Duchess of York, who lived here for the last 26 years of her life. She was a colourful and historically important figure, the mother of two kings of England, Edward IV and Richard III. In her later years she suffered great tragedy with the deaths of her son, Edward IV in 1483 and then two of her grandsons in the Tower of London. Two years later in 1485 Richard III was killed at the battle of Bosworth. After Cicely's death in 1495 it seems that the castle was no longer inhabited. The story does not, however, end here. The royal connection continued. Even in a ruined state, the castle has remained a focal point of the town.

Although the castle was of great significance, we must not forget the town that had grown up at the other end of Castle Street. The town's prosperity derived from trade along the highway as well as from the castle. Berkhamsted has the triangular market place and burgage plots typical of a medieval market town, but it is uncertain exactly when these were laid out. The ancient road from Windsor, which reaches the High Street at the bottom of Chesham Road, may originally have continued straight on to the castle, rather than veering to the right to skirt round St Peter's Church and then down Castle Street. Property boundaries recorded on the 1839 tithe map support this theory.

The town's historic parish church, St Peter's, also raises unanswered questions. It would appear that the parish was carved out of the parish of St Mary, but the date is uncertain. No part of St Peter's Church predates the 13th century. The oldest part, the chancel, dates to c1200. No archaeological survey has been made of St Peter's, but it is possible that an earlier smaller church stood on the same site. Irregularities in the ground plan, and portions of a mid 12th-century font found during restoration work in 1871, support this theory. Documents of the 13th and 14th century mention a church of St James, with a graveyard; it is referred to as an ecclesia (church) rather than a capella (chapel), indicating parochial status. It is also significant that the annual fair was held on the Feast of St James until Victorian times. Other records suggest that St James's stood near the sorting office at the junction with St John's Well Lane.

THE HIGH STREET AND THE PARISH CHURCH c1955 B407003

Further along the High Street is another easily identified scene. Cycling two-abreast would be difficult today, and a computer shop has replaced the Co-op (right), reflecting the needs of a differing age!

Fact File

St John's Well was a spring, which appears in medieval records; in the 19th century it was still reputed to cure sore eyes, a 'holy well'. The water ran down St John's Well Lane to the river until it dried up in the mid 20th century.

The new church, St Peter's, seems to have been deliberately placed in a prominent position close to the market place and the approach to the castle. Geoffrey Fitz Piers, Earl of Essex, holder of the castle at the time, was the founder of the church, one of the largest in the county. Its grandeur also reflects the flourishing wool trade in the town at this period.

The south side of the High Street was higher and drier, and it was here that the wealthier properties of the medieval town were to be found. On the other side were the stalls, shops and shambles of the traders. It appears that the later medieval lay-out of the town was the result of a deliberate plan initiated by Geoffrey Fitz Piers, and that it was contemporaneous with the building of St Peter's Church and Castle Street. At about the same time he founded two hospitals, the Hospital of St John the Baptist and the Hospital of St John the Evangelist. It is likely that the second was at the eastern end of the town. Both were dissolved in the 1520s, and the revenues used as part of the endowment for Berkhamsted School.

We are looking back past St Peter's Church towards the Baptist Church. The buildings themselves have changed little, only their uses.

HIGH STREET c1955 B407013

THE
SWAN HOTEL
CHESHAM & BRACKLEY
BREWERIES LTD.
SWAN
CLEANING, DYEING.
& VALET SERVICE

By the early 13th century, the market and centre of trade was situated much where it is today. Shops were originally little more than stalls, but these became more like open-fronted shops by the end of the medieval period. The range of trades was extensive. The timber trade was important, and carpenters, woodmen, wood turners, dish makers and tool makers lived here. Wine was produced. A taxation list of 1290 gives a wide range of trades: brewer, lead burner, carpenter, trades of the leather industry, fuller, turner, butcher, fishmonger, barber, archer, tailor, naper, miller, cook, seller of salt, huntsman, and many more.

A WOODCUT SHOWING SHEPHERDS AND SHEEP 1510
ZZZ04901 (Berkhamsted Local History and Museum Society)

Wool merchants demanded good, sound fleeces. Centuries before William Cooper invented his powdered sheep dip, shepherds powdered and washed their flocks.

Wool merchants were flourishing, and were doubtless the most important beneficiaries of Henry II's charter of 1156. They were to be 'free of all tolls and duties whithersoever they go, whether through England, Normandy and Spain.' We know from a letter from King Edward III, dated 1332, that John le Fuller, John Gentilcorps, Ralph de Cheddington and William le Shephard, all men from Berkhamsted, had business interests in Flanders. They were prosperous men, even lending money to the king. Berkhamsted's woollen industry ceased to exist in early Tudor times.

So what remains today of Berkhamsted's medieval town, apart from the castle and St Peter's Church? Opposite the church at 125 High Street is a two-storied timber-framed building with a north range parallel to the street and a wider wing. In this wing is one bay of a 14th-century open hall; its plan suggests that there was once a second

THE MEDIEVAL CLOTH TRADE

In the reign of Richard II there was a subsidy of four pence per broadcloth. Every piece was inspected by the alnager, an official who examined the cloth. If it was up to standard, he gave it his seal. It was illegal to sell unsealed cloth. In 1316 a Berkhamsted exporter, Adam Puff, lost a large cargo of wool worth £1,200 when the Admiral of Calais captured his ship bound for Antwerp. The ensuing 'trade war' lasted for several years.

bay of the same size. This was a very large house. Possibly it had some manorial function, or accommodated royal officials. It was altered and extended in subsequent centuries. Dean Incent's House at No 129 belonged to Robert, secretary to Cicely, Duchess of York. The oldest part of the remaining building is 15th-century.

173 High Street (see ZZZ04918, below), once thought to be Victorian, incorporates timbers felled in the period 1277 to 1297, which makes it the earliest known surviving jettied urban building in England. Its true date was only discovered in 2003. It is a two-storey, timber-framed building with a crown-post roof. It is no doubt part of a much larger house, which has since disappeared. It is thought to have been a three-bay cross wing to an aisled hall. Perhaps it was the home of a wealthy wool merchant.

The oldest part of the Swan, 139 High Street, has roof timbers partly of the 14th century; behind this the rear wing retains parts of an early 15th-century open-hall house. 207-209 High Street dates from the late 15th century. The centre bay has a crown post roof. Other medieval buildings may lurk behind later façades, especially on the southern side of the High Street. There is undoubtedly more to discover.

THE SOUTH SIDE OF THE HIGH STREET 1890 ZZZ04918 (Berkhamsted Local History and Museum Society)

Behind the apparently Victorian façade (centre, 'Established 1869'), survives the earliest known jettied urban building in England.

CHAPTER TWO

A CASTLE IN RUINS

Neils
Mr. FINLAY
CASTLE
wine merchants
CARPETS
FURNITURE
CHINA & GL
PART EXCHANGE
SANDEMAN
PORT

THE CENTURY following the demise of the castle saw economic decline, with loss of royal favour. The castle was abandoned by the court, and the buildings fell into disrepair. Nevertheless, Berkhamsted Castle still appears in royal records. In 1503 the Under Keeper sent a buck to Windsor for the queen of Henry VII. Subsequently, the Manor of Berkhamsted was granted in turn to three of Henry VIII's wives, Catherine of Aragon, Anne Boleyn, and Jane Seymour, but the castle was in too ruinous a state to be lived in. Berkhamsted's position worsened when Henry VIII granted Hemel Hempstead a market charter, which enabled that town to develop at the expense of Berkhamsted.

Berkhamsted fought hard to maintain its position, and all was not doom and gloom. Less is heard about important personages and more about the ordinary people of the town. Important events during Tudor times indicate some recovery, which is reflected in the following extract from the writings of John Leland. On his travels through the area (1535-1543) he wrote: 'Berkhamstede is one of the best markette townes in Hartfordshire and hathe a large street meetly well builded from north to south, and another but somewhat lesser, from the west to the east, where the river renneth.'

THE RIVER BULBOURNE, MILL STREET 2005 ZZZ04946 (Ken Wallis)

This photograph was taken not far from where the river once powered the Upper Mill.

During the 16th century a market house was erected about a hundred yards west of St Peter's Church. It was built of brick and timber and covered with tile, and lofted overhead; it housed a corn market. The ground floor was open, and perhaps housed stalls. Near by was a butter market. Near the market house were butchers' shambles, divided into several stalls and covered with tiling. This market house remained until 1854, when it was destroyed by fire.

In 1618 James I gave Berkhamsted a charter of incorporation, by which the town became a free borough, with a corporation. The inhabitants became 'one body corporate and politic'. The corporation consisted of a bailiff and twelve burgesses. It was permitted to make bye-laws for the borough, to impose fines, penalties, and imprisonment, to have an extra market day every week and two additional fair days annually, to maintain a prison, to collect market tolls, and to hold a court of record once a month and a court of pied poudre to deal with petty offences on fair days.

Fact File

A court of pied poudre (from 'pied poudreux', old French for 'dusty feet') was held during fairs to give speedy justice, while the dust of the fairground was still falling from the feet of pedlars and others involved in disputes.

A DRAWING OF THE 16TH-CENTURY MARKET HOUSE c1835 BY J BUCKLER (1770-1851) ZZZ04902
(Berkhamsted Local History and Museum Society)

Berkhamsted Corporation met in the Court House, which dates from the Tudor period. Here were heard 'all pleas, actions, suits or offences against the laws and liberty of the manor', and here also the corporation kept standard weights and measures. The Court House exists today, although much altered. Early documents refer to it as the Church House or Town Hall. The corporation derived no lasting benefits from its privileges, and fell into abeyance in the 1660s.

The Dissolution of the Monasteries in the reign of Henry VIII had a significant effect on Berkhamsted and its religious foundations, especially on the community of the Bonhommes at Ashridge. In 1539, when the Act suppressing larger monasteries with an annual value of over £200 became law, Ashridge was surrendered. The last rector, Thomas Waterhouse, bequeathed his monastic vestments to the churches of Quainton, where he was rector, Hemel Hempstead, where he is buried, and Great Berkhamsted.

Henry VIII, like his poet laureate, Skelton (who wrote: 'A pleasanter place than Ashridge it harde were to finde'), liked Ashridge and hunted there at least once. With the Dissolution, Ashridge was not left to fall into ruin, and seems to have been spared the destruction of books and works of art that many monasteries suffered. It remained in Crown ownership for nearly 40 years until Queen Elizabeth disposed of it. Ashridge was one of the homes of Henry's three children, Edward, Mary and Elizabeth. Elizabeth retired there when Mary became queen and spent many hours embroidering 'some of ye childe bed things' for the child that was never born to her sister. In 1553 Mary ordered Elizabeth's arrest, suspecting her of being implicated in the Wyatt rebellion; she sent commissioners to take her to the Tower of London, but Elizabeth was said to be too ill to travel, and no case could be proved against her.

Robert Incent, secretary to Cicely, Duchess of York, lived in Dean Incent's house opposite St Peter's Church, and his son, John, was probably born there. John never lost interest in the town of his birth; when he became 'president and cheafe' of the Brotherhood of St John the Baptist, he secured agreement to appropriate lands and rents for a school, and a schoolmaster was appointed. As Dean

THE CORPORATION COAT OF ARMS

A reminder of the former Corporation of Berkhamsted is the present-day coat of arms, granted to the bailiff and burgesses nearly 400 years ago. The design was chosen 'upon deliberate consideration that the glory of that place hath proceeded from the ancient castle there ... In a shield, or (gold), a triple tow'red castle azure, within a border of Cornewall, viz, sables besanted.'

of St Paul's he realised the threat to the Brotherhood from the Dissolution, and in 1541 he obtained a licence from the king to found and build a school in Berkhamsted for 144 pupils and to endow it with lands to the value of £40 a year.

THE LATER YEARS OF ASHRIDGE

In 1604, Ashridge passed to Thomas Egerton, James I's Lord Chancellor, who restored and extended the monastic buildings. His son was created the first Earl of Bridgewater. His direct descendants held Ashridge for two centuries. The third Duke of Bridgewater, Francis Egerton, born in 1736, was only twelve when he succeeded his brother. He concentrated on building canals and moved to Lancashire. Ashridge became neglected. When his canal projects proved successful he returned to Ashridge, where he planned to build a great house, but death intervened. He is buried in Little Gaddesden Church with the epitaph: 'Memorable among those who were honoured in their generation and were the glory of their times.' A better-known memorial to him is the tall column above Moneybury Hill, the Bridgewater Monument, from the top of which are extensive views of the surrounding countryside.

DEAN INCENT'S HOUSE c1955 B407043

BERKHAMSTED SCHOOL, THE EARLY DAYS

'Not without ye healpe of ye town and country ... he [Dean Incent] builded with all speed a fair schoole large and great all of brick very sumptuously ... When the saide Schole was thus finished (1544) ye Deane sent for ye cheafe men of ye towne into ye school where he kneeling gave thanks to Almighty God'. (Haulsey of Berkhamsted). Richard Reeve was then placed in 'ye seate there made for ye schoolmaster.' After Dean Incent's death, the school was incorporated by Act of Parliament under the name of 'the Free Schole of King Edward the Sixte in Berkehampstedde'. The school prospered, but its history during the Civil War and the subsequent Protectorate reflected the troubles in the country at large. The 18th century saw the rise and fall of its fortunes and a long, expensive lawsuit. It was not until the headship of the Rev Dr John Dupré (1789-1805) that it revived. This 18th-century print shows the Old Hall, 1544, still in use today.

BERKHAMSTED SCHOOL c1750 ZZZ04903 (Berkhamsted Local History and Museum Society)

Many new buildings in the 16th century were built with bricks and stone from the ruined castle. This was particularly true of Berkhamsted Place, built by Sir Edward Carey, Keeper of the Queen's Jewels, on the hill above the castle. It is thought that the present entrance across the moat into the castle grounds was cut through at this time so as to make it easier to carry away stone from the castle. In 1580 Elizabeth had leased Carey the Manor of Berkhamsted, which included the ruined castle and the deer park, at the nominal rent of one red rose. Sir Edward never lived in his new house in Berkhamsted, preferring to live in Aldenham, so the house was let to his brother Sir Adolphus Carey and later to his son.

We cannot leave Berkhamsted Place without mentioning the Great Barn at Castle Hill Farm, the home farm of Berkhamsted Place. The barn, probably 16th-century or earlier, is a weather-boarded building with timber framing - much of this original framing survives. In recent years its condition has deteriorated, but plans are afoot to convert it into housing.

BERKHAMSTED PLACE

Since Berkhamsted Place belonged to the Crown, it was sequestrated during the Civil War. It is described in a survey of Crown lands in 1650. It was a grand building, built in a courtyard plan. After a fire in 1661, more than half of the house was demolished and rebuilt by John Sayer. Most of what remained was demolished in 1967, and part of the grounds built over. At this time many worked stones from the castle, possibly from the chapel, were found. Some of the great house and gardens still remain at the end of a private drive at the top of Castle Hill.

THE HIGH STREET c1965 B407113

We are approaching the town centre. On the left is the Swan Inn, on the right is Graball Row.

There are few other 16th-century buildings left in Berkhamsted, only 296-298 High Street, a two-storey house of the early 16th century, altered in the 17th century; the Crown Inn, originally built in the late 16th century; Edgeworth House, Northchurch, a 16th-century house of timber framing on brick foundations; the George and Dragon public house; and Rosemary Cottage, originally a farm, both also in Northchurch.

The change and turmoil of the 17th century was reflected in events in the town. The people of Berkhamsted showed their independent spirit in the first 'Battle of Berkhamsted Common'. The town once so reliant on the prosperity generated by the castle supported Cromwell during the Civil War, and paid for it economically at the Restoration of Charles II.

When the Duchy of Cornwall had enclosed 300 acres of the Common in 1618 to 'improve' the land, there had been little opposition amongst the townsfolk of Berkhamsted, but the reaction of the commoners and some of the tenants was different, particularly those of Northchurch. A compromise was reached with a warrant dated 20 February 1619. The 300 acres were to be enclosed, but the Duchy

Fact File

The Duke of Cornwall (afterwards Charles I) came to Berkhamsted in 1616. 20 horsemen met him at Brickhill Green and escorted him down Chesham Road and Castle Street, where he stopped to hear a speech of welcome in Latin by 'one of the Schollers of the free Schole.' He then proceeded to Berkhamsted Place, where he hunted in the park. It was not until the 20th century that a Duke of Cornwall was to visit Berkhamsted School again.

THE DODDERIDGE AND NORDEN SURVEYS

In his survey of 1607, John Dodderidge details the usage of the Common: 'the inhabitants & tenantes of this Mannour dwelling within Barkhamsteede & Northchurch have used by auncient custome to have perceive and take in the Fryth and other waste groundes herbage & pannage, Bushes, furzes, stubbes and fearne for their necessary uses for their landes and tenements and common of pasture in the sayd Fryth and other the Common & waste groundes of the said Mannour for all manner their Cattel, at all tymes of the yeere, sans number.' This survey, together with that of John Norden and Edward Salter in 1616, had been carried out to determine 'all the circuits, Buttes, Bounds and Lymittes of this Mannor (ie Berkhamsted) and upon what other Mannors, Lordshippes or Landes the same doth bound'; they provide a fascinating insight into 17th-century Berkhamsted. Some of the common rights were still exercised until well into the 20th century.

promised that 'noe more should be inclosed afterwards.' Resistance continued, however.

On the night of 3 July 1620 a crowd of about 200, armed with farm implements and weapons 'did in most warlike, riotous and unlawful manner march, ... and repayer unto the royal park in Berkhamsted ... Did in most outrageous manner cutt, breake, and sawe down all the pales, postes, and Rayles wherewith the sayd Parke was invironed and inclosed.' The first 'Battle of Berkhamsted Common' had begun. Following this, 25 men were arrested. The strongest opposition came from Northchurch. The ringleader was William Edlyn, who was described as a 'mann of troublesome disposition.'

This enclosure, and the release in 1628 of over 1,000 acres of the park for cultivation, brought some benefit to the economic life of the town. Many people could now start their own farms or smallholdings, and it brought employment for those who had suffered because of the decline of the wool industry.

In 1639 the Crown once more needed revenue, and the Duchy of Cornwall proposed the enclosure of a large portion of the Common. Again there was powerful opposition, largely from Northchurch tenants, and several were arrested. Petitions and counter-petitions followed, and eventually the House of Lords ordered that 'the Prince his Highnesse shall quietly and peaceably hold and enjoy the said landes within the mannours aforesaid'. Those arrested were pardoned and bound over not to re-offend. Unrest, however, continued. As a result this enclosure was destroyed and the fences were not re-erected. In 1654 the tenants' and inhabitants' Common rights were confirmed by the Commissioners. Two more centuries passed before another attempt was made to enclose the Common.

Berkhamsted's support for the monarchy waned in the second quarter of the 17th century. The passing of the king and queen through Berkhamsted in 1636 went largely unnoticed. The corporation record book acknowledged 'the blame that was layd upon us by neglecting our formal attendance and presents to the kinge and queene.' In 1638, whether from poverty or lack of inclination, Berkhamsted's payment of the £25 levy for Ship Money was 'longe behynde'. Berkhamsted, like much of Hertfordshire, was staunchly Parliamentarian during the Civil War. No battle took place in the district, but the townspeople often had to provide quartering and provisions for soldiers.

One of Cromwell's soldiers was Daniel Axtell, born in 1622 in Berkhamsted. His father, William, was chief burgess and a town clerk. Daniel was apprenticed to a London grocer, but gave up his trade and joined Cromwell's army. In 1648 he was captain of the guard at the trial of Charles I.

The execution of Charles I was greeted with horror not only by all good Royalists but also by many Parliamentarians among the citizens of Berkhamsted. Not only did Anne Murray, of Berkhamsted Place, describe the execution as 'that execrable murder never to be mentioned without horror and detestation', but a Berkhamsted man, Nathan Paine, declared that he regretted having fought with the Parliamentarians and added that the execution was 'the most horrid murder that ever any history made mention of.' For this he and two other local men, Thomas Aldrich and Nathan Partridge, were brought before the bailiff and chief burgesses by an order from the Council of State, but they were acquitted and continued to take an active part in the life of Berkhamsted. Aldrich was bailiff in 1655 and Paine was a churchwarden in 1658.

Daniel Axtell received his just deserts. After the Civil War he had served in Ireland, but in 1656 he resigned his commission and returned to Berkhamsted, not to the house in which he had grown up, but to Berkhamsted Place, the previous home of the Murrays. In 1660 he was arrested and tried as a regicide, and sentenced to death. His end at Tyburn, according to legend, was dramatic: the driver of the cart refused to play his part in the hanging, and the common hangman had to be called. Axtell declared he had followed the cause of the Lord: 'I ventured my life freely for it, and now I die for it.'

Fact File

An entry in the churchwarden's accounts for 1660 reads: 'the happy yeare of King Charles the Seconds restauration to his government.' Church bells rang, and fireworks were let off. The parish spent 10s on a 'barrell of beare' for the celebrations and 15s 2d on powder and match. The bell ringers received £1.

At this time a number of Berkhamsted people either on grounds of religious belief or for economic reasons left the town to seek their fortunes in America. Daniel's brother, Thomas, was one of these. He went to New England, where his descendants founded a family association. Members of another local family, whose descendants still live in Berkhamsted, also went out to New England, to Connecticut. William Pitkin, son of a headmaster of Berkhamsted School, and later his sister, Martha, both founded dynasties which have played a prominent part in American history.

THE MURRAYS OF BERKHAMSTED PLACE

Thomas Murray was secretary and former tutor to Charles I. His daughter, Anne, figured in a successful plot to send the young Duke of York (later James II) to Holland. The duke was rowed down the Thames to a riverside house and dressed as a girl. Anne obtained the garments from a tailor, and was among those who bade him farewell. Anne was deprived of her interest in the lease of the Manor of Berkhamsted, but in 1685 received a pension of £100 a year from James II, a belated recognition of her help in his escape from London in 1648. Murray Road, close to Berkhamsted Place, is named after the Murray family.

BERKHAMSTED PLACE, AFTER THE ORIGINAL DRAWING BY C I TYLER c1700
ZZZ04904 (Berkhamsted Local History and Museum Society)

Drawn for Edward Sayer, who was the second son of John Sayer.

John Sayer, who rebuilt Berkhamsted Place after a disastrous fire, is better known today for his gift to the poor widows of Berkhamsted. All who pass by the almshouses at the bottom of Cowper Road can read for themselves the inscription: 'The Guift of Iohn Sayer Esqr 1684.' John was a kinsman of the Rev Joseph Sayer, Rector of Northchurch from 1675 to 1693, and died at Berkhamsted in 1682. He is buried in St Peter's Church. Head cook to Charles II, he was with him in exile during the time of the Commonwealth.

John Sayer bequeathed £1,000 for building almshouses and for the relief of the poor. His widow, Mary, augmented the bequest by £300. An almshouse was designed with twelve rooms for six poor widows at a cost of £269. The balance was invested in land, and the income from it was devoted to the needs of the almswomen and other poor parishioners. Candidates had to have lived ten years in the parish and to be 'of good fame, constant frequenters of divine service as by law established in the Church of England, and aged 55 years at least.'

SAYER'S ALMSHOUSES c1905 ZZZ04919 (Berkhamsted Local History and Museum Society)

The Royal Oak Inn next door was demolished in 1908 to make way for the Gas Company showrooms, and is now a restaurant.

THE PLAQUE ON SAYER'S ALMSHOUSES 2005
ZZZ04947 (Ken Wallis)

A number of other 17th-century houses survive, among them the Bull, not originally a public house; Boxwell House, which is late 17th- or early 18th-century; and close by, the Lamb, still a public house, an inn in earlier times. On the road to Chesham we come to Kingshill, now the National Film Archive - the oldest parts of this are 17th-century. In Castle Street we find the Boote, a timber-framed building dated 1605. It was a tavern until 1920. Not far from the Old Mill Hotel, in Bank Mill Lane, is the Old Cottage, built in 1647.

Marmaduke Rawdon wrote rather unkindly in 1657: 'Barkhamsteed; this is a longe market towne and antient. Thir is little in this towne worth the seeing, only the free schoole and the ruines of the castle.'

GORSESIDE

A map of 1612 marks houses on the edge of Berkhamsted Park abutting onto the Common, close to where Castle Village, a residential complex for the elderly, now stands. These houses were on the old drovers' road from Aldbury to Hemel Hempstead, and were close to the road to Nettleden and Ashridge. Only one house remains today, Gorseside, originally a farmhouse, latterly used as the sales office for Castle Village. It was scheduled for demolition to make room for five luxury homes. Thermographic imaging has confirmed it to be 17th-century. The house, listed Grade II in 2004, is typical of a house that has been altered through the centuries to meet the needs of its occupants.

SPARROWS HERNE TRUST MARKER, 352-356 HIGH STREET 1987 ZZZ04920 (Eric Holland)

In the 18th century, during the coaching era, Berkhamsted's strategic position on the old Akeman Street meant that the town became a staging post on the road from London to Aylesbury and the Midlands. In July 1762 the Sparrows Herne Turnpike Trust held its first meeting at the King's Arms, Berkhamsted. The trust was responsible for the 27 miles of highway from Bushey Heath to Aylesbury, via Watford, Berkhamsted and Tring. The nearest tollgate to Berkhamsted was at Newground, beyond Cow Roast. The trust had power to 'amend, widen, alter and keep in repair' the highway. A painted iron post bearing the name of the Turnpike Trust can still be seen at the corner of Park Street. Tolls were collected every six or seven miles. Cattle and sheep were an important source of revenue for the trust when they were brought from Wales or the Midlands to markets in London. Drovers often rested their animals in paddocks off the road, for example behind the Goat Inn in Three Close Lane.

Men employed to improve the highway were paid 6s a week. In 1821 James McAdam was appointed as main surveyor for the trust, and instigated improvements of the road surfaces. In 1823 toll rates were as follows: 4½d for a horse-drawn coach, 1½d for a laden pack horse, 1d for an unladen beast, 10d per score for droves of oxen or cows, and 2½d per score for calves or pigs. In 1832 tolls

THE GOAT INN 1985 ZZZ04921 (Eric Holland)

were raised further, and a system of hired labour and paid officials was established. With no proper drainage system, the roads were often waterlogged in bad weather.

In 1792, at the height of stagecoach travel, one company was charging 8s 'inside' and 6s 'outside' for the fare from Berkhamsted to London. By 1836 the cost had been adjusted to 12s for sitting inside and 2s for outside. The Universal British Directory of 1791 lists the various possibilities of coach travel at the time. From the Swan Inn one could travel four times a week to the Bell in Holborn. There was a Tring coach passing through, stopping at the King's Arms three times a week. A coach to Banbury passed through, another to Birmingham, and later another to Kidderminster - altogether quite a comprehensive service!

A number of Berkhamsted's old inns survive, although some are no longer licensed. The Queen's Arms, first recorded in 1607, relinquished its licence in 1968. The Goat, first recorded in 1782, was a drovers' inn. It was rebuilt in 1841. The Crown, next to the Swan, was built in the late 16th century and

THE SWAN 2005 ZZZ04948 (Ken Wallis)

This ancient house, no longer an inn, today provides accommodation for young people and provides facilities for the youth of the town.

first mentioned as an inn in 1734. The King's Arms, next to the Crown, was recorded from 1716 and flourished as a coaching inn during the late 18th and early 19th centuries, hosting public events and the petty sessions, and acting as a post office.

The prosperity of the coaching era brought several larger houses to the High Street; some of these used the structure of earlier buildings. These include, on the south side, the Red House, Sydney House, now Barclays Bank, and Exhims in Northchurch.

THE KINGS ARMS c1890 ZZZ04922
(Berkhamsted Local History and Museum Society)

On the north side were other 18th-century houses, some quite substantial. One of these, Pilkington Manor, was demolished in 1959 - only the name and a replica of the portico remain on the recently built flats. The Dower House also dates from this period. 218 High Street, incorporated in Mackay's department store, is 18th-century, and so are a number of houses in Castle Street.

This century saw the building of several large mansions on the edge of the town; sadly few remain today. On the approach from the east was the Hall, demolished in the 1930s, remembered now by the various road names with Hall Park in them. At the top of Highfield Road stood Highfield House, also demolished in the 1930s. Near Ashlyns School is Ashlyns Hall, built in the late 1780s for Matthew Raper - this house still stands today. A little further away on the road to Chesham is Haresfoot, now a school. Damaged several times by fire, little remains of the original house.

POLLY PAGE

Polly Page, born in 1787, was the innkeeper's daughter at the King's Arms. Louis XVIII, exiled from France, came to England and set up his court at Hartwell House near Aylesbury. He always changed horses at the King's Arms, and usually contrived to see pretty Polly. With the fall of Napoleon in 1814 Louis returned to France, where Polly is said to have visited him. Gossip was unkind to Polly, and she published a denial of any impropriety. It was later said of her she had been 'as remarkable for meeting with extraordinary circumstances as for maintaining an irreproachable character in the course of her life.' Polly became innkeeper on the death of her father in 1840 and received Queen Victoria and the Prince Consort when they changed horses there.

Thomas Bourne (1656-1729), Master of the Company of Framework Knitters, bequeathed £8,000 to build and endow a charity school in Berkhamsted for 20 boys and 10 girls. He was not a resident, but often visited his sister, Sarah Rolfe. Bourne directed that the boys were to be taught to 'read English, write and cast accounts', while the girls 'after being perfected in reading English' were to 'do such work as the churchwardens should think fit for such girls to learn.' The school opened in 1737, but it was not until 1761 that the girls were taught to write, and then only in their last year at school. In 1854 General Finch of Berkhamsted Place defrayed the cost of rebuilding the school. In 1875 the boys and girls were transferred to the National School and the traditional uniform was discontinued, although bonnets and caps were worn until 1914.

The town was a centre of religious non-conformity from the 17th century, and about a fifth of the population were dissenters. It was not, however, until the early 18th century that chapels were built. The first Baptist chapel was built in Water Lane in 1722, and had a burial ground. It was later enlarged. Although there were several Quaker families in the town, there was no Meeting House here until 1818. Congregationalists can be traced back to 1780, when the first meetings were held in the parlour of a lace merchant in Castle Street. In the 1790s their first chapel was built in Castle Street, on the corner of what was later Chapel Street. In the following century, as the congregation grew, two further chapels, each larger than its predecessor, were built on the same site.

It would not be right to leave this century without reference to two very different individuals, William Cowper, the poet, and Peter the Wild Boy. William Cowper, (or 'Cow Per' as he is known locally to distinguish him from William Cooper, an important 19th-century citizen), the son of John Cowper, Rector of St Peter's and chaplain to George II, was born in Berkhamsted in 1731. His happy early childhood was sadly shattered by the death of his mother. He was educated first at a school in the High Street, in what is now part of the department store, Mackays. After the death of his mother he was sent to school in Markyate, where he was cruelly bullied, and later to Westminster School. He last visited Berkhamsted in 1759, three years after the death of his father, and wrote then: 'There was neither tree, nor gate, nor stile in all that country to which I did not feel relation.'

Fact File

Tucked away on the southern edge of the Common is Moor Cottage, built in 1774 by the Berkhamsted Vestry as the Pest House for the isolation of those with smallpox and other infectious diseases. Inoculation decreased the need for a Pest House, but even as late as 1856 it was still being let to tenants on the condition that they receive infectious patients when required. Now a private house, an inscription inside bears witness to its earlier use.

THE BOURNE SCHOOL COAT OF ARMS ZZZ04923 (Berkhamsted Local History and Museum Society)

Fact File

There are three coats of arms above the door of the former Bourne School: that of Thomas Bourne, that of the town, and that of General Finch.

HIGH STREET c1955 B407034

We are at the crossroads, looking west. William Cowper attended school in the second building from the right.

Until recently the only memorial to William Cowper was the stained glass in the east window of St Peter's Church, inserted in 1872. All the panels have quotations from his Olney hymns, and one of them shows the poet at his prayer desk with his tame hares. It is now difficult to gain access to this window. For the millennium year a new window, in which his hares also feature, was erected as a memorial to Cowper. Two roads, Cowper Road and Gilpin's Ride, commemorating his poem 'John Gilpin', remind us of this poet.

Peter the Wild Boy, of German origin, lived in the parish of Northchurch for nearly 60 years. He was the subject of scientific interest, is mentioned by Daniel Defoe, and was used by Jonathan Swift as a model for his Yahoos in 'Gulliver's Travels'. He is referred to by Charles Dickens in 'Edwin Drood' and 'Martin Chuzzlewit'. Peter was found in 1725 in a field near the town of Hamelin in Germany. He was almost naked, and appeared to have been living wild. He was brought to England, apparently at the request of the Princess of Wales, later Queen Caroline. All attempts to teach him to speak failed, as his memorial in St Mary's, Northchurch states: 'But, proving incapable of speaking or of receiving any instruction, a comfortable provision was made for him by Her Majesty at a farm house in this Parish where he continued to the end of his inoffensive life.' Peter lodged at Haxter's End Farm, now demolished, with James Fenn, and later with his brother, Thomas Fenn, at Broadway Farm.

BERKHAMSTED RECTORY, COWPER'S BIRTHPLACE, 18TH CENTURY ZZZ04905
(Berkhamsted Local History and Museum Society)

This was demolished c1850 and a new rectory was built on the same site. In the 20th century the present rectory was built lower down the hill.

And so we leave 18th-century 'Great Berkhamsted ... [which has] most pleasant environs with high and hard ground, full of hedge rows, pastures and arable ... it extends itself far in handsome buildings, and a broad street.' ('A Gentleman', 1762). According to the Universal British Directory of 1791, the chief trade was bowl turning, shovel and spoon making, with a large quantity of lace made by women. The Directory shows a virtually self-sufficient community, and gives the names of the different traders and gentry. But the town stood on the threshold of change. By the turn of the century the canal had arrived, and Berkhamsted was to enter a new era of growth and prosperity.

Fact File

Peter the Wild Boy once strayed as far as Norfolk, so Mr Fenn had a leather collar made for him with a brass ring with the inscription: 'Peter, the Wild Man from Hanover. Whoever will bring him to Mr Fenn at Berkhamsted, Hertfordshire, shall be paid for their trouble.' This collar still exists, and is preserved at Berkhamsted Collegiate School.

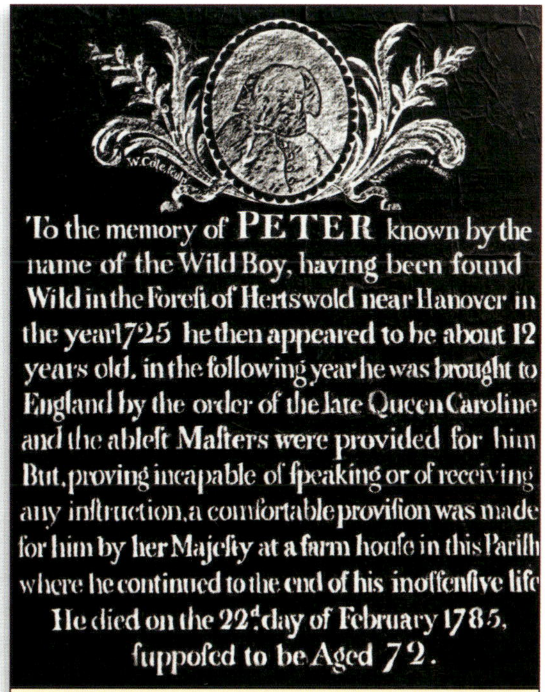

A RUBBING OF PETER THE WILD BOY'S MEMORIAL IN ST MARY'S CHURCH, NORTHCHURCH 1785
ZZZ04906 (Berkhamsted Local History and Museum Society)

THE LACE INDUSTRY

In the 18th century, pillow lace making was a thriving cottage craft. With gaily-beaded bobbins, women worked on pillows to which were attached pricked parchment or cardboard patterns, glittering with pins to make a framework for the threads. The same patterns were used over and over again. From the large quantity of halfpenny tokens bearing the words 'Pay at Leighton, Berkhamsted or London', it would appear that Berkhamsted was an important centre of the lace trade. The tokens were issued by Chambers, Langston, Hall & Co, lace merchants and haberdashers of Leighton Buzzard and London. One of the firm's partners lived in Berkhamsted. The tokens bear the date 1794, and fulfilled a need when small change was scarce. In the 19th century this industry was largely replaced by straw plaiting, but continued in isolation into the 20th century.

LTD.
NATIONAL
ROVINCIAL
BANK
Fashions
WARDS
WARDS
SALE

CHAPTER THREE

'HOPES OF A FLOURISHING FUTURE'

AT the start of the 19th century, Berkhamsted was little different in size from the medieval town. Little building had taken place away from the triangle formed by the High Street, Castle Street and Mill Street, apart from a few farmhouses and mansions on the outskirts. The town remained clustered around the parish church and the market house, close to where Tesco now stands, with coaching inns nearby on the southern side of the street. Many people lived in yards leading off the High Street; some of these can still be seen. At the side of St Peter's Church, Castle Street led down past the Grammar School to the ruined castle beyond, an idyllic setting for courting couples.

The first major development was the canal, begun after the formation of the Grand Junction Canal Company in 1793. An army of 'navvies' descended on the district, living in camps and shocking the more staid citizens with their drunken orgies. Connecting Birmingham with the Thames, this canal is the longest wide-gauge canal in Britain, with a total of 108 locks. The Berkhamsted section was costly. Between Boxmoor and the Cow Roast alone, 20 locks were needed to raise barges through the Chiltern Gap. The Grand Junction Canal was opened from Brentford to Tring in 1798 and the entire route in 1805, 200 years ago this year.

ST PETER'S CHURCH AND CASTLE STREET 2005 ZZZ04949 (Ken Wallis)

Work on the Tring summit, which had to carry the canal to 405 feet above sea level, involved digging a cutting over 1½ miles long and over 30 feet deep in places. Every boat crossing the Tring Summit uses 200,000 gallons of water to achieve this height. To safeguard supplies for the canal in dry weather, the Wendover Arm was built as a feeder branch. Additionally, reservoirs were built near Tring.

To take the road over the canal, humpback bridges were built. At the end of Castle Street the road was raised by several feet, with the effect that a row of cottages on the left-hand side became known as the 'sunken cottages'. These were demolished in 1964 and replaced by the Berkhamsted School Sanatorium.

The canal was an immediate success, and brought great benefit to Berkhamsted's economy. Wharves were built along the canal, and new industries grew up which required bulk transport of materials, such as timber, grain, and flour and malt from local mills. The barges returned from London laden with soot and dung as fertiliser for farms. For the first time, coal reached the district in quantity and at a reasonable price, although local people burned wood and furze for years. All boats were horse-drawn until the introduction of 'steamers' in the 20th century. Blacksmiths prospered, and canal-side taverns, such as the Boat, the Crystal Palace, and the Rising Sun had a flourishing trade.

A yard for building barges and other boats was established between Castle Street and Raven's Lane at Castle Wharf. A barge called the 'Berkhampstead Castle' was built in the town in 1801, and used for carrying hay to London and returning with coal. By 1826 the yard was owned by John Hatton, who also dealt in coal and salt. It was taken

THE SUNKEN COTTAGES c1890 ZZZ04924
(Berkhamsted Local History and Museum Society)

The Temperance Hotel (behind the horse and cart), founded 1879, later became St George's, one of Berkhamsted School's day houses.

over by William Costin in about 1882, and carried on until about 1910. The wharf still exists today, probably the last remaining boat-building wharf in the south of the country, although now under threat.

The other 'newcomer' to Berkhamsted, which was markedly to alter the lives of its citizens and add to the growth and prosperity of the town, was the railway. Surveys for the line had started as early as 1825. Two routes from London to the north had been proposed: one via Oxford and Banbury, the other by Rugby and Coventry. George and Robert Stephenson, whose advice was sought, favoured the latter route.

> **Fact File**
>
> *In Victorian times and in the first half of the 20th century many a Sunday school treat started with a trip by horse-drawn canal boat from Castle Street to Newground; the children then continued on foot or by wagonette to the Bridgewater monument above Aldbury for a picnic.*

POCOCK'S SHOEING FORGE (A CLARIDGE PHOTOGRAPH) c1860 ZZZ04925
(Berkhamsted Local History and Museum Society)

The photographer William Claridge lived opposite the forge at the east end of the High Street.

Landowners objected to railways crossing their estates. Among these was Lord Brownlow at Ashridge, who spoke vigorously in the House of Lords against the project, declaring that the case for the London & Birmingham Railway Bill did not warrant 'the forcing of the proposed railway through the land and property of so great a proportion of dissentient landowners.' Despite his pleas, the London & Birmingham Railway Act received the royal assent in May 1833.

An army of workmen was brought into the town by Cubitts, the contractors. Lodgings had to be found for them. At one time as many as 700 were said to be working on the railway. There were cockney and Irish labourers, bricklayers from the Midlands, and miners from the north of England. Many married local girls. Among these men were a few Wesleyan Methodists, who introduced Methodism to Berkhamsted.

The building of the railway through Berkhamsted and Northchurch proved even more difficult than the building of the canal. Not only had the engineers and navvies to contend with geological difficulties, but they also had to cope with Berkhamsted Castle, the outer moat of which abutted on the planned route. That they managed to do this without the help of any excavating machinery is a remarkable feat of 19th-century engineering. Unfortunately, this was not done without the loss of human life. Parish registers show that seven men were killed while building the Berkhamsted section of the railway, and in the parish of Northchurch there were at least four fatalities.

THE CANAL AND THE RAILWAY c1840 ZZZ04907 (Berkhamsted Local History and Museum Society)

To take the line past the castle it was necessary to build a high embankment over part of the outer moat, and an enormous number of bricks had to be used to secure a firm foundation. A temporary bridge was thrown over the road to Whitehill, and earth dug out to make the Sunnyside cutting was taken by cart and wheelbarrow to complete the building of the embankment. The building of the Northchurch tunnel was an equally difficult undertaking.

The line was opened as far as Tring in October 1837, and through to Birmingham in September 1838. Berkhamsted's first station, almost opposite the end of Castle Street, was a fine building praised for its Elizabethan style of architecture. In the early years, three up and three down trains stopped at Berkhamsted on weekdays. First class passengers paid 8s for a single journey to London, travelling in covered upholstered carriages. Second class passengers paid 6s 6d to travel in coaches open at the sides. A third track was added in 1857-59; travel had by that time become a little cheaper, 5s first class, 3s 6d second class, 2s 4d third class. Then, one could travel from London to Berkhamsted in 53 minutes, a journey little longer than that of today.

In about 1840 the Castle Hotel was built at the end of Mill Street, facing the original station. It had good stabling for barge horses, and served both the station and the canal. It closed as a hotel in 1968, and now forms part of an attractive group of flats.

In 1846 the London & Birmingham Railway had been taken over by the London & North Western Railway. Further growth in freight traffic led to the construction of

Fact File

A steam locomotive, the 'Harvey Coombe', was brought by canal to Bourne End. A temporary track was laid to transport truckloads of soil from the Northchurch tunnel and the Billet Lane cutting to build the embankment between Bourne End and Boxmoor. Henry Weatherburn, its driver, sometimes gave local residents a free ride before the railway was officially opened.

THE FIRST RAILWAY STATION, BY J BUCKLER
ZZZ04908 (Berkhamsted Local History and Museum Society)

This bridge still remains today. Traces of this station, which was opened in 1837, can be seen in the brickwork on the castle side of the bridge.

a fourth track in 1875. At the same time the present station was built with extensive sidings, replacing the old goods yard between the original station and Gravel Path. The old station continued in use as a wood-turner's workshop and brush works, and did not disappear until the 1930s. There is some remaining brickwork next to the railway bridge on the old site. The present station retains the original booking hall, some of the wooden platform canopies, and a private waiting room built for Lord Brownlow on the north side of the station.

From early times timber had been an important industry in Berkhamsted. By the mid 18th century, both Berkhamsted and nearby Chesham were noted for turned wooden products. Originally a trade of small artisans, it later took advantage of the bulk transport opportunities provided by the canal, becoming one of the town's most important industries in the 19th and early 20th centuries.

JOB EAST'S FIRST TIMBER YARD (A WILLIAM CLARIDGE PHOTOGRAPH) c1860
ZZZ04926 (Berkhamsted Local History and Museum Society)

These were the humble beginnings of Job East. Here we can also see the house called Waverley and the Black Horse.

The most prominent timber merchant was one Job East. He came to Berkhamsted in 1840 from Chesham to take over a small shovel-maker's and turner's business, which was started in the 18th century by a man named Austin. His yard was at the eastern end of the town, next to the Black Horse (now an Indian restaurant). East produced a variety of wooden tools and furniture including chair frames, bowls, tent pegs, brooms, shovels, and hurdles. Initially he employed only ten men, and used a sawmill with horse-gearing attached. Later he used steam sawmills. The Crimean War brought contracts for supplying the army with lance poles and tent pegs and led to major expansion. Following a fire in 1888 the timber works was moved to a site in Gossoms End. At this time under the direction of Job's son, Cornelius, the firm was described as 'the largest single-handed business of its kind outside London.'

As well as East's there were several other timber yards, the largest of which was Key's, by the canal in Castle Street. This was replaced in the 20th century by Alsford's, which closed in the early 1990s. Now, where new flats are, the only reminder of the timber trade is the Canadian totem pole, a present to Alsford's from the state of British Columbia in the 1970s.

THE TOTEM POLE 2005 ZZZ04950 (Ken Wallis)

EAST'S LATER YEARS

The East family dynasty lasted until 1917, when Catherine East, Job's granddaughter, sold the company, which continued to trade as East & Sons of Gossoms End. The site near Stag Lane was extended from 1½ to 6 acres. The manufacturing East's undertook was mainly for large Government contracts. In 1932 the company won a substantial contract to make 202 lock gates for the Grand Union Canal. The timber yard finally closed in the early 1990s, and the Stag Lane area was developed as a light industrial estate.

An offshoot of the timber industry was brush making. There were two local firms, T H Nash in George Street, which continued until the 1920s, and a larger firm, Goss brushworks, in the High Street close to Cross Oak Road. It closed in the late 1930s. In late Victorian times these employed a hundred people, mainly girls and women.

Until well into the 20th century Berkhamsted was very much a country town. In 1822 William Cobbett reported that the lands of this part of Hertfordshire were 'very fine; featuring a red tenacious flinty loam, upon a bed of chalk, which makes it the very best corn land we have in England.' The lands of Kitsbury Farm ran close to the town centre - sheep grazed on meadows where later Cowper Road and Torrington Road were built, and a threshing barn stood on the corner of Rectory Lane. There were two water mills in the town grinding locally produced grain. Berkhamsted was a largely self-sufficient community. Until a few years ago, sheep from the Berkhamsted Hill Research Station could still be seen grazing on the slopes above the castle. Many of the town's historic farmhouses, such as Cross Oak and Kitsbury, are now remembered only in street names.

Henry Lane founded his nursery business in 1777, specialising originally in hedging plants, which flourished on Berkhamsted's fertile ground. By 1851 his son, John, had built large greenhouses on either side of St John's Well Lane and was employing a staff of over 30. He later specialised in roses and vines, which he exported to France, Belgium and Germany. Henry Lane & Son is perhaps best remembered today for the apple Lane's Prince Albert, which was first produced in the town.

WELL FARM 2005 ZZZ04951 (Ken Wallis)

This is one of Berkhamsted's few remaining farms. This photograph was taken looking towards the common.

LANE'S PRINCE ALBERT

The original Lane's Prince Albert apple tree was in the garden of a house called The Homestead, 250 High Street, demolished in 1958 and replaced by shops. Thomas Squire, a Quaker, who lived at The Homestead, often experimented with seeds and cuttings. On 26 July 1841 he planted out a small apple tree after cheering Queen Victoria and the Prince Consort as they drove through the town. Thomas named the tree the Victoria and Albert, and in due course it bore excellent fruit. Lane's marketed it as 'Britain's latest apple' and renamed it Lane's Prince Albert. Unfortunately, the original tree was cut down when the house was demolished.

From the mid 19th century the firm operated on three different sites. A map of 1878 shows that the Home Nursery had land in St John's Well Lane, Park Street and the area of Cross Oak Road. On the present-day Canal Fields it had a rose nursery. Lane's also established Balshaw Nurseries at Potten End and Broadway Nurseries at Bourne End.

Fact File

Those of you who heed the notice 'Freshly picked plums for sale' and drive up the steep lane to Broadway Orchard every summer are buying plums from one of the remaining fruit orchards of Lane's Nurseries.

THE CANAL, THE FORMER LOWER MILL WHARF 2005 ZZZ04952 (Ken Wallis)

Sadly, the prolonged depression following the First World War began the decline of the business, although the nurseries in Potten End did not close until the 1950s. A small nursery still exists on that site. Part of the Home Nursery near St John's Well Lane was used by Bulbourne Nurseries until the 1970s.

Another industry for which the Bulbourne valley provided ideal conditions was the watercress industry, a short-lived industry in the history of the town. In 1883 The Berkhamsted Times congratulated Mr Bedford on converting, at great cost and labour, 'dirty ditches and offensive marshes to pleasing watercourses in which grows a most healthy product. He has created a new industry which affords employment to many men.' At its peak the industry sent approximately two tons of cress a day by train from Berkhamsted to London, Liverpool and Manchester. Similar quantities from Bourne End and Chesham were also dispatched from our station. The main cress beds in the town were situated between Billet Lane and St John's Well Lane. Three generations of the Bedford family grew cress in Berkhamsted; two Harry Bedfords, father and son, were succeeded by Dennis Bedford, and his uncle, Frank Bedford, grew watercress at Dudswell

THE VIEW FROM GRAVEL PATH RAILWAY BRIDGE c1865 ZZZ04927 (Berkhamsted Local History and Museum Society)

Here we see the town still clustered mainly round the church and the High Street. The first pair of houses in Chapel Street has just been built.

and Northchurch. The local cultivation of watercress survived until the 1960s.

An 1839 directory listed brewing as one of the main industries. Large quantities of beer were consumed. Initially publicans had their own brew houses, but gradually some began to provide beer for several houses, thus creating larger breweries. The former Swan Brewery in Chesham Road first supplied only the Swan Inn. By 1839 it was being run by the Foster family, who later built a second maltings in Chapel Street, which is used today by local Scouts - on the side wall can be seen the words 'Foster's No 2 Malting.' Fosters also supplied the Brownlow Arms, at the corner of Ravens Lane and Chapel Street, the Rose and Crown, and the Pheasant at Northchurch, as well as other hostelries outside the town. The Swan Brewery closed down in 1897.

Another, much larger, local brewery was Locke & Smith's, which was in Water Lane. At the peak of its activity it supplied nearly 40 local licensed houses. This brewery was taken over by Benskins of Watford and closed shortly before the First World War.

Dwight's Pheasantries, established in 1734, was an important local industry for almost 250 years. It is thought to have been the largest and oldest of its kind in England. Members of the Dwight family reared game for many generations, the business handed down from father to son. William Dwight, who developed the business in the 19th century, had three sons, one of whom lived in The Pheasantries, a house at the top of Ivy House Lane. The other brothers farmed Little Heath Farm in Potten End, producing grain as feed for the pheasants.

Every year 20,000 young pheasants were raised, and pheasants and their eggs exported in large quantities to every part of the world. By the 1940s, Dwight's had 3,000 brooding hens hatching pheasants' eggs, and in 1965 the laying pheasants produced over 100,000 eggs in a single laying season. Dwight's Pheasantries is no more, and in the late 1970s a housing development, Hunters Park, was built on a small part of the site. Ivy House Lane is still known today as Dwight's Lane by locals of the older generation.

We have already mentioned James Wood's ironworks, set up in 1826. Born at Marlin Chapel Farm, James later lived with his family at Monk's House, now the Café Rouge. In the nearby yard he started making and repairing iron and wirework. James soon began to take on larger contracts for greenhouses, ornamental gates and garden furniture. He did work for the leading landowners of the day, especially the Rothschilds and the Brownlows. The iron and glass-fronted showroom built about this time formed a familiar part of the shop premises until they were destroyed by fire in January 1973. Many still remember the smoke and flames leaping into the sky and the explosions as pots of paint ignited in the blaze. Following the fire, the present garden centre was founded. In 1996 Wood's celebrated 170 years of trading.

We must not forget the young animal doctor, son of a farrier, who arrived from London by carrier one evening in the early 1840s with his few belongings in a black carpet bag - among them, so the story

J WOOD & SON'S PREMISES AUGUST 1971 ZZZ04928 (Eric Holland)

The building to the left of the picture was destroyed in the 1973 fire.

goes, were his pestle and mortar. This was William Cooper, born in 1813 in the village of Clunbury in Shropshire, whose invention of sheep dip was to take the name of Berkhamsted to almost every corner of the globe. We do not know why he left his work in Montgomery and came to Berkhamsted. Perhaps he chose it for its proximity to London. In 1849 he was one of the first to qualify at the Royal College of Veterinary Surgeons, which had received its royal charter in 1844.

At first he had an uphill struggle, making his rounds on foot, although by 1845 he owned a horse and chaise. He kept in close touch with blacksmiths, butchers, and dealers, who were likely to know of any sickness on farms. Once established,

HALSEY'S COTTAGE, CASTLE STREET c1890
ZZZ04929 (C H Sills)

This is reputed to be where William Cooper first lived in the early 1840s. The house was demolished in the 1930s when Manor Close was built.

Cooper's practice developed rapidly. By 1851 he had engaged William Wilson as his assistant. Cooper was concerned about the scourge of scab in sheep, and sought a remedy. He eventually formulated an arsenic and sulphur sheep dip in powder form, the first successful product of its kind. He later passed his veterinary practice over to William Wilson so that he could concentrate on the manufacture of sheep dip.

In 1852 a small factory was built in Ravens Lane. Initially, horse-powered mills were used for grinding the ingredients, and kilns for boiling up the mixture. Steam-powered machinery was introduced in 1864; the business expanded rapidly. The works, between Ravens Lane and Manor Street, was extended several times. This later included a printing department, which was to become the Clunbury Press. By the 1870s the company was exporting the product overseas. Behind the Lower Works in the High Street was a wharf for the unloading of sulphur, arsenic and coal, and the loading of packets of Cooper's Dip for transport to the London docks. Sibdon Place in the High Street, west of Ravens Lane, was built in 1869 for senior employees. William Cooper lived first in a cottage in Castle Street, later in the High Street, until he built Clunbury House in Ravens Lane. At the time of his death he was living at The Poplars, 71 High Street, previously occupied by John Lane of Lane's Nurseries.

WILLIAM COOPER'S FIRST FACTORY c1850
ZZZ04909 (Berkhamsted Local History and Museum Society)

WILLIAM COOPER AND HIS FACTORY

One of Cooper's first apprentices, George Gomm, described Cooper: 'In appearance, Mr Cooper was most striking, standing over six feet in height and well-built, with a keenly intellectual face and broad, deep forehead, surrounded by a wealth of iron-grey curls ... Though quickly roused, he was most ready to forgive and his kindliness to the poor was shown in many ways.' Of some of the working practices in the early days he writes: 'The dressing of the sulphur was done by means of a machine called the 'Joggler', invented by George Dean. This was a long, flat sieve in a deep box, moved backwards and forwards at a high speed by a wrench ... for some considerable time, this crank was turned by hand, but it was eventually geared to the old mare's roundabout. The speed was considered so great and dangerous that a warning notice was placed on the door.'

SHEEP DIP BEING LOADED AT LOWER WORKS WHARF c1910
ZZZ04930 (Berkhamsted Local History and Museum Society)

The man on the far right is Eric Preston.

THE POPLARS 2005 ZZZ04953 (Ken Wallis)

William died in May 1885. He is buried in the family vault in Berkhamsted cemetery, and there is a memorial window to him in the north transept of St Peter's Church. After his death the business was taken over by his nephews, and the later decades of the century saw considerable expansion of overseas trade. The business continued to flourish for many more years, diversifying and adapting to the changing needs of the 20th century.

In the 19th century the chief cottage industry was straw plaiting, carried out predominantly by women and young girls. The tools for this were a straw splitter, made of wood, bone or iron, which held cutters resembling miniature wheels with a varying number of razor-sharp spokes. In the middle of each wheel was a cone, on which each straw was centred before it was pushed through the cutter and sliced into the required number of splints. The sliced straws were pressed flat in a small mangle, which was usually fastened to the kitchen door. Then the plaiting started - the workers usually held the straws in their mouths. The most popular local varieties of plait were China Pear, Rock Coburg and Moss Edge. The finished plait was cut into lengths of 20 yards.

In Berkhamsted and nearby villages children were sent to straw-plaiting schools - at one time there were three plaiting schools in Bridge Street alone. Sometimes the children were taught in the dark to accustom them to working without looking at the plait. Once a week the finished plait was sold to agents of Luton and Dunstable hat makers at straw plait markets in Berkhamsted, Tring and Hemel Hempstead. Changes in fashion and in attitudes to child labour as well as foreign competition led to the demise of the industry by the end of the century.

Fact File

Sibdon Place is named after the little hamlet of Sibdon Castle, close to Clunbury in Shropshire. William Cooper's grandparents Thomas and Ann Cooper were married there in 1784. Their eldest son William and his wife Sarah lived in Clunbury, where William Cooper of sheep dip fame was born in 1813.

The Victorian era saw the extension of educational opportunities. At the beginning of the 19th century, apart from the sons

HIGH STREET c1955 B407018

We are looking east over the Kings Road junction.

of the privileged few who could afford to educate their children privately or at one of the grammar schools, other children had little opportunity to receive any sort of education. In Berkhamsted we had the Bourne Charity School and the Grammar School. The latter had a somewhat chequered history. Whereas the Reverend John Dupré had ensured that a wide curriculum was taught, thus attracting more scholars, his son, Thomas, who succeeded him as headmaster in 1805, shamefully neglected his pupils.

Repeated representations to the Court of Chancery made by Augustus Smith of Ashlyns Hall and others finally forced Thomas Dupré to resign in 1841. The new headmaster, the Reverend Edward Wilcocks, and the usher, George Scott, were made members of the governing body. It was made compulsory for senior masters to live at the school. The school reopened in 1842 with 43 boys. Under Wilcocks's successor, the Reverend J R Crawford, numbers dropped again. It was not until the appointment of Dr Edward Bartrum in 1864 that the school began to flourish. For the first time the numbers exceeded Dean Incent's original target of 144 pupils.

BERKHAMSTED SCHOOL, SCHOOL HOUSE c1960 B407047

This shows the original Tudor building. It is no longer known as School House. The memorial to Mary Smith-Dorrien still stands in the churchyard.

As well as being a successful scholar, Dr Bartrum was a keen sportsman, and he persuaded the governors to lease ten acres of ground from Lord Brownlow of Ashridge for a sports ground. It was during Bartrum's tenure that Founder's Day was initiated on 23 July 1885. Dr Bartrum has been described as 'the real second founder.'

During the last years of the 19th century and the first decade of the next the school was in the capable hands of Dr Thomas Fry. He initiated many improvements, and created the Castle Campus of Berkhamsted Collegiate School, as we know it today. At his own expense he bought Overton House at the corner of Chesham Road and land behind it, on which a new senior boarding house, St John's, was built. In 1889 he launched a fund to build a school chapel and a gymnasium; he also secured a county council grant to help him build a 'science school', a very innovative project for the time.

A local shopkeeper, Henry Nash, secured an agreement to finance a local school for girls. In 1887 a Board of Governors under the chairmanship of Sir John Evans acquired the lease of the empty Bourne School building. The Berkhamsted Girls' Grammar School was formally opened on 11 May 1888 under the headship of Miss C Disney, with 14 pupils. The girls had the use of tennis courts in the town and a swimming pool at the Waterworks.

BERKHAMSTED SCHOOL CHAPEL (ARTIST UNKNOWN) c1900 ZZZ04910
(Berkhamsted Local History and Museum Society)

In 1897, when Miss Harris became headmistress, there were 80 pupils at the school, and larger premises were required. The governors proposed that the Boys' School should acquire a suitable site and lease it back to the Girls' Grammar School. The new building in Kings Road was opened in 1902.

BERKHAMSTED SCHOOL CHAPEL

The school chapel was dedicated in June 1895, and was designed by Mr C H Rew, a Berkhamsted architect. The design was inspired by the Venetian church of Santa Maria dei Miracoli. It, together with Deans' Hall, completed after Dr Fry had left to take up his post as Dean of Lincoln in 1910, is a fitting memorial to his achievements and those of Dean Incent.

BERKHAMSTED SCHOOL CHAPEL AND THE LYCH GATE c1920
ZZZ04931 (Berkhamsted Local History and Museum Society)

THE BERKHAMSTED GIRLS' GRAMMAR SCHOOL AT THE BOURNE SCHOOL 1897
ZZZ04932 (Berkhamsted Local History and Museum Society)

The building is discreetly decorated for Queen Victoria's diamond jubilee.

Fact File

One of the pupils at the Girls' Grammar School at the turn of the century was Clementine Hozier, who later became Lady Churchill. She lived for several years with her mother and sisters in the High Street close to Rectory Lane.

PARK VIEW SCHOOL, FORMERLY THE BRITISH SCHOOL 1971 ZZZ04933 (Eric Holland)

Augustus Smith was not only intent on improving the educational facilities for the better off. In 1833 he persuaded the Vestry to establish a British School. This non-denominational school was opened in 1834 on the site of the old parish workhouse, at the bottom of what is now Park View Road. In 1871 the school was enlarged, and it took infants from 1894. The school closed in 1971, with the introduction of middle schools, but the premises were used by Social Services before being demolished in 1984.

In 1838 the Church of England built a National School onto the back of the Court House, with a house next door for the master. It had classrooms for 238 children and is marked 'Courthouse School' on the

THE COURT HOUSE c1955 B407046

The Court House was renovated c1980.

1879 Ordnance Survey map. The children from the Bourne School transferred to the National School in 1875. Infants' schools were opened in Chapel Street and Gossoms End. Further afield, schools were opened at Potten End (1856) and Northchurch (1864). In 1897 the Victoria School for Boys was built in Prince Edward Street. A few years later, the Victoria Girls' School was built next door. The classrooms at the Court House were then vacated.

NORTHCHURCH & GOSSOMS END NATIONAL SCHOOL (ARTIST: H HAWKINS) 1857
ZZZ04911 (Berkhamsted Local History and Museum Society)

The smaller building to the right, the Infants' School, was used by Cubs and Scouts until well into the 1970s.

Fact File

Before these schools were set up, many boys and girls were taught to read and write at Sunday Schools. The first was established in June 1810 by Joseph Hobbs, pastor of the Baptist Church, with the support of the Congregational minister. A few months later the Church of England also opened Sunday Schools in Berkhamsted and Northchurch.

SCHOOL FEES AT THE NATIONAL SCHOOLS

Extract from 'Dawn of the Day', the parish magazine, December 1878: 'As so many children of a superior class are now taking advantage of the excellent education given at the National Schools, the Managers have resolved to increase the Fees in every case, except that of the labouring poor. This will be done according to the means of the parents, on a scale ranging up to 9d, which, according to the Government calculation, is about the amount, which the maintenance of each child costs at the National Schools. There will of course be no difference in the education given. The School was founded for the poor, and whilst the Managers welcome the children of those who are better off, this must always be remembered.'

THE COURT HOUSE AND THE PARISH CHURCH c1960 B407052

The Court House is still the site of many parish and town activities. The building on the extreme left was built for the master of the National School.

BERKHAMSTED PLACE, THE CASTLE (PUBLISHED BY J GREEDY) 1856 ZZZ04912
(Berkhamsted Local History and Museum Society)

Berkhamsted Place was frequently referred to as the Castle in the late 19th and early 20th centuries, and is listed as such in some of the later censuses.

Adults at this time also had educational opportunities, most notably through the Mechanics' Institute. In 1845 the Institute's inaugural lectures on 'The Philosophy of the Human Mind' were held in the National School. The Institute's first reading room opened in a house in the High Street, now part of Mackays. The reading room moved later to 21 Castle Street and then to a room in Nash's yard, where the Civic Centre now stands. When the new Market House and Town Hall was built in 1859 it included a reading room for the Mechanics' Institute.

From that time onwards the Town Hall became the home of the Mechanics' Institute, which was able to expand its facilities and activities. It held a programme of lectures and annual exhibitions in the Town Hall to encourage local artists and craftsmen. Substantial prizes and medals were awarded for the best entries. An 1890 extension to the Town Hall provided the Institute with billiards, snooker and card rooms. In the reading room was an impressive library of books, daily newspapers and other journals. The programme of evening lectures was comprehensive, ranging from chemistry, woodwork, history and elocution to shorthand.

The Mechanics' Institute played an important part in Berkhamsted life for nearly 130 years. After dropping 'Mechanics' from its title in 1930, it ceased to function in

THE MECHANICS' INSTITUTE READING ROOM c1920 ZZZ04934 (Berkhamsted Local History and Museum Society)

Seated at the table is Albert Edward Loosley, Registrar of Marriages for the sub-district of Berkhamsted.

the early 1970s. Two tables, the newspaper lectern and a board exhorting the people of Berkhamsted to 'Come and join the Institute' survive. The Institute Room is now part of the Clock Room. It is hoped that a permanent exhibition in memory of Percy Birtchnell, a founder member of the Berkhamsted Local History Society and a long-standing member of the Institute, will soon record its history.

The market had never really recovered from the difficult times of the Cromwellian period. The Universal Directory of 1791 refers to it as 'much decayed', and George Lipscomb on his travels in 1802 refers to the town as 'shabby and much decayed - the market house propped up by not a few rough posts.' Some residents considered the Tudor market house an unsightly obstruction. One night in August 1854 the market house was burnt down; whether by accident or intent, we shall never know.

Two months later a public meeting was held at the King's Arms to discuss the building of a new market house 'suitable to the increasing prosperity of the town.' William Hazell, a grocer, secured a site for £823 and public subscriptions were invited for the new building. Four architects were invited to submit plans. At first the majority supported plans by E F Law of Northampton, but Lady Alford, of Ashridge, persuaded them to accept those by Edward Buckton Lamb, who had done restoration work at Chequers and restored churches at Wendover and Aston Clinton. Earl Brownlow, Lady Marian Alford, General Finch of Berkhamsted Place, and Mrs Smith-Dorrien of Haresfoot contributed large sums. A Grand Bazaar was held in the castle grounds to raise the rest. The Town Hall and Market House was formally opened in August 1860.

A QUAKER MURDERER

One of those involved in setting up the Mechanics' Institute was John Tawell, a Quaker, who lived at the Red House. In the five years he lived in Berkhamsted he took an active part in the affairs of the town. In 1841 he married a widow, Sarah Cutforth. The community was deeply shocked when he was arrested for murder, being convinced it must be a case of mistaken identity. At Aylesbury Crown Court it was revealed that he had earlier poisoned his mistress, one Sarah Hart, in Slough. Tawell was sentenced to death and hanged in Aylesbury Market Place in 1845. He was the first murderer to be caught as a result of a message transmitted by the electric telegraph.

During this period there was a gradual improvement in living standards. In 1849 the Great Berkhampstead Gas, Light & Coke Co Ltd was set up to provide street lighting. The townspeople raised £106 towards street lights and piping, thus ensuring that the hard-pressed Vestry only had to pay for the gas itself and any maintenance required. The first gas was manufactured in a works at the junction of Water Lane and the Wilderness. It used coal delivered by canal until later in the 19th century, when coal was delivered by rail along a track laid from the sidings to the gasworks. A single-storey brick building survives, now used by the Collegiate School.

In 1906 the gas works moved to Billet Lane. Here an old horse called Ruby was later used to haul the coal in small wagons along a single rail track. Part of this track can still be seen today. Ruby was later succeeded by a small diesel engine, which remained in service until the Berkhamsted gas works closed in 1959. Gas for the town was then supplied through a pipeline from Boxmoor. In 1958 sodium lighting replaced the gas lighting in Berkhamsted High Street. Natural gas was supplied to the town in the 1970s.

Electric light was used in the town at the Mechanics' Institute's Grand Exhibition in 1886, but it was the beginning of the next century before the Chesham Electric Light Company supplied electricity to the town. Many houses did not have electric light until after the Second World War, and one or two houses retained gas lighting until the early 1980s.

Until the second half of the 19th century, Berkhamsted people were reliant on wells for their water supply. A few of these still exist. In 1864 the Great Berkhampstead Waterworks Company Ltd was set up. The waterworks in the High Street (near the Town Hall) included baths, and were erected at a cost of £6,500. A small steam engine was used to raise water from a deep bore, twelve inches in diameter, to a high-level reservoir at Kingshill. Later a low-level reservoir was built in Green Lane, where Priory Gardens now is. In the following century the increasing population led to the building of the water tower in Shootersway. It was not until the final years of the 19th century that an effective sewerage system was established.

ADVERTISEMENT FOR JAMES BOWLER, COAL MERCHANT c1880 ZZZ04913
(Berkhamsted Local History and Museum Society)

THE TOWN HALL c1910 ZZZ04935 (Berkhamsted Local History and Museum Society)

The square building next but one to the Town Hall is the waterworks.

'HOPES OF A FLOURISHING FUTURE'

The Rev John Wolstenholme Cobb, of St Peter's, in his second lecture to the Mechanics' Institute in 1855 on the subject of 'The History and Antiquities of Berkhamsted', concluded with the words: 'Our canal, our railway, our gas, and last, though not least, our Mechanics' Institute, are all proofs of advancement in civilization. They are evidences of the liberal spirit, which pervades our town and neighbourhood, and they are tokens of essential prosperity. They are improvements which in themselves call for real congratulation, and the more so because they fill us with hopes of a flourishing future ... PROSPERITY TO THE TOWN OF BERKHAMSTED.' Cobb produced a printed version of his two lectures, copies of which can still be obtained.

The history of Ashridge in the 19th century is of particular importance. It was the 7th Earl of Bridgewater who built the present house between 1808 and 1814. The great building, designed in Gothic revival style by the architect James Wyatt and completed by his nephew, Jeffrey Wyattville, still stands today. The Earl died childless in 1823, but his widow continued to live at Ashridge until her death in 1849. The property passed to Viscount Alford, son of Earl Brownlow, who lived only until 1851. His widow, Lady Marian Alford, reigned over Ashridge until her son Edward came of age in 1863. She was a powerful figure, who not only did a great deal for the village of Little Gaddesden, but also exerted influence over the affairs of Berkhamsted. Edward died at the age of 24, to be succeeded by his younger brother, Adelbert.

Adelbert's wife, Lady Adelaide, was a great hostess, and her hospitality brought royalty and many distinguished visitors to Ashridge, including the Shah of Persia in 1889. Queen Mary was a frequent visitor. Lady Brownlow died in 1917 and Lord Brownlow in 1921. They were the last private owners of Ashridge.

ASHRIDGE, THE NORTH FRONT IN 1853, A PRINT BY GEORGE DANCER THANE ZZZ04914
(Berkhamsted Local History and Museum Society)

Deer are still plentiful on the Ashridge Estate today.

THE SHAH OF PERSIA AT ASHRIDGE IN 1889 (PHOTOGRAPH BY WILLIAM COLES, WATFORD)
ZZZ04936 (Berkhamsted Local History and Museum Society)

The Shah is pictured here with the Duke of Clarence and Lord and Lady Brownlow.

In 1761 the Manor of Berkhamsted had been leased by the Duchy of Cornwall to the Duke of Bridgewater, predecessors of the Brownlows. In 1863 Lord Brownlow's trustees succeeded in buying for £144,546 the whole of the Manor of Berkhamsted from the Duchy, with the exception of the castle. It was not long before the new Lord of the Manor threatened to enclose stretches of Berkhamsted Common. Lord Brownlow's agent, William Paxton (nephew of Sir Joseph Paxton of Crystal Palace fame), informed the Berkhamsted Vestry that he was willing to give the town a central recreation ground 'as a just and liberal compensation in lieu of existing trivial outstanding claims on the common.' The recreation ground would have extended from Mill Street to Billet Lane, between the Bulbourne and the railway, plus a few acres south of the river at Gossoms End. Ten of the total 43 acres were scheduled for allotments.

Many of the townspeople considered this a bargain, preferring a central recreation ground to heathland on the hilltop a mile away, and 413 people signed away their rights. Not everybody considered their common rights to be 'trivial'. Among those who objected

THE COMMON 2005 ZZZ04954 (Ken Wallis)

were Augustus Smith of Ashlyns Hall, then living on the Isles of Scilly and recently elected MP for Truro, and Thomas Whately, a local surgeon.

Early in 1866 Lord Brownlow proceeded with the enclosure. An order for fencing was placed with James Wood, the Berkhamsted iron founder, whose workmen erected two miles of iron railings. One third of Berkhamsted Common - the central portion - was enclosed. This prevented traffic from passing along tracks from east to west and excluded people from exercising their common rights. Augustus Smith discussed the matter with George John Shaw-Lefevre, Chairman of the Commons, Open Spaces and Footpaths Preservation Society. It was decided that the fences should be forcibly removed, as an assertion of common rights. The second 'Battle of Berkhamsted Common' was about to begin.

A trainload of labourers, armed with hammers, chisels and other implements, was brought down from London to Tring Station; joints in the railings were loosened, and the fences were uprooted. Legal proceedings were initiated against Augustus Smith; he began a counter action, which dragged on for three years until judgement was given in his favour. The Master of the Rolls declared that a right of common pasture existed, and a right to cut furze, gorse, fern and under-wood for fodder and litter, but not the right to cut timber for house repair and so on. The 'right of recreation' was negated. However, the people of Berkhamsted continued to roam over the

A BAPTIST SUNDAY SCHOOL OUTING c1890 ZZZ04937 (Berkhamsted Local History and Museum Society)

Fact File

Mr William Fisher, who lived to be over 90, worked for Messrs Wood at the time of the enclosure, and recalled the events as an old man. He helped to erect the fencing, 'and some time afterwards I was detailed off to clear away the twisted remains of the fences.' He recounts vividly the return of the navvies to Berkhamsted Station, where they were paid for their night's work.

Common, and do so to this day.

Evidence of the increase both in the prosperity as well as the size of the town is shown in the new church building of the period. A new Baptist church was built in 1864 in the High Street at the corner of Ravens Lane to meet the needs of an ever-growing congregation. In 1867 a large Congregational Chapel, which replaced the 1834 building, was built at the corner of Chapel Street and Castle Street. This was demolished in 1974 and replaced by the William Fiske House for the elderly. A United Reformed Church was built on the site of the former churchyard.

The buildings for the Methodists were more modest in size. In 1854 the Wesleyan Methodists built a chapel in Prospect Place, now Highfield Road, but after a short time moved to Cowper Road. In 1867 a chapel was built for the Primitive Methodists in the High Street almost opposite Kitsbury Road. In 1953 the Wesleyan and the Primitive Methodists merged.

In the last decades of the 19th century two

THE CONGREGATIONAL CHAPEL OF 1867, CASTLE STREET c1870 ZZZ04915
(Berkhamsted Local History and Museum Society)

new Anglican congregations were established in temporary iron buildings to cater for the expanding populations in the Kitsbury and Sunnyside areas. All Saints' Church, Kitsbury, was dedicated in 1905, and Sunnyside in 1909. In 1976 All Saints' agreed to share its premises with the Methodists.

In common with many Anglican churches in the 19th century, St Peter's Church saw some significant restoration work. In 1820 Jeffrey Wyattville carried out some rather unsatisfactory alterations, but later William Butterfield made some substantial improvements, although not without destroying some of the original features. He transformed the exterior appearance of the church by re-facing the church with flint.

THE PARISH CHURCH c1955 B407044

Fact File

Flint gathered from the demolition of some of the interior dividing walls of St Peter's was stored in Matthews' builders' yard and later used for the building of Sunnyside Church.

772 EBH

SUNNYSIDE CHURCH AND ALLOTMENTS 2005 ZZZ04955 (Ken Wallis)

We must not forget that for many, poverty was never far away. In the 18th and early 19th century the workhouse had been a wretched thatched building on the site of the later British School. The Reverend George Nugent, who lived at The Red House in the High Street, 'moved to compassion towards those poor unfortunate creatures' obliged to live in the old workhouse, bequeathed £1,000 for a new workhouse in 1830.With the setting up of the Board of Guardians in 1834, this became the Union Workhouse. It remained in use until 1935, when all the inmates were transferred to Hemel Hempstead. It was replaced by the parade of shops, Kitsbury Parade.

By the 1840s the Bridewell, the local prison, was in a dilapidated state and was no longer secure. In 1843 alterations were made to 'render the place fit for a police station to which prisoners might be remanded before commitment, but it would not be fit for prisoners under any sentence, however short.' In 1894 the building was demolished. At the same time Kings Road was widened, and a new police station was built on the same site. This in turn was demolished in 1972 to make room for the present building.

The Local Government Act of 1888 had transferred local functions of justices of the peace to county councils, and in 1894 another act set up borough and urban district councils. In 1898 the Berkhamsted Urban District Council was formed. To begin with, the council met fortnightly in the workhouse. Mr Thomas Penny, solicitor, was appointed clerk at £50 per annum, and Mr E H Adey, who also worked for other local authorities, was paid £75 from the council as Inspector of Nuisances, £2 as Inspector of Dairies and Cowsheds, £3 as Inspector of Canal Boats and £20 as Surveyor.

Many people from different walks of life left their mark on 19th-century Berkhamsted. Dr Thomas Whately, a local doctor and surgeon, who lived in Egerton House, is perhaps best remembered for his gift of the great west window in St Peter's Church.

Sarah Littleboy, a well-to-do Quaker woman who lived in Boxwells, visited the inmates of the workhouse regularly, held Bible meetings for the poor women of Berkhamsted in her kitchen, and concerned herself with the welfare of the children in the British School. She was born in Amersham, the daughter of a miller, and married William Littleboy of Bourne End Mill. She moved to Boxwells after the death of her husband. As well as bringing up a large family she wrote poetry. She is buried

RAVENS LANE LOCK c1905 (PHOTOGRAPH BY NEWMAN) ZZZ04938 (Berkhamsted Local History and Museum Society)

Ravens Lane Lock looking west. Compare this with the contemporary photograph ZZZ04966 on page 110.

in the Meeting House graveyard in the High Street.

Thomas Read was born in Tring in 1826, the son of a pit sawyer. The family moved to Berkhamsted in the early 1830s and Thomas attended the British School. He was a founder member of the Mechanics' Institute, and in 1869 he founded the Berkhamsted and Northchurch Working Men's Club, and was its president for many years. He worked in the timber trade, and soon set up his own business with a steam-powered sawmill. He represented Berkhamsted on the County Council from 1892 to 1895, and was chairman of many local bodies. After his death in 1897 a clock was erected on the Town Hall in his memory. His obituary in the Gazette described him as 'the most remarkable man in Berkhamsted, the most successful man of business, the most public-spirited business man, the most prominent example of a self-made man.' His family tomb can be seen in the former graveyard of the Congregational Chapel.

No doubt football had been played in the town for some time, but it was in the last years of the century in 1891 that competitive football began in the district with the formation of the West Herts League.

THE TOWN HALL c1965 B407114

The White Hart, to the right of the Town Hall, was demolished in the early 1970s.

Two local teams were founder members, Berkhamsted School and Berkhamsted Sunnyside. By 1895 the Sunnyside team had been disbanded, and Berkhamsted Town FC was formed. In only its second season the club became league champions for 1896-97, and in the 1898-99 season they were competing in the Herts County League as well as the West Herts League. Over the years the team has had varying success, and now plays in Division I East of the Southern League.

Records of competitive cricket date back even further. In 1835 there were two annual derby fixtures between Tring and Berkhamsted, one played at Tring Park and the other on the Common. In the 1860s several notable games took place at Haresfoot, the home of Colonel R A Smith-Dorrien, and by 1870 organised cricket was played regularly on Butts Meadow. The first official fixture list we have of the Berkhamsted Cricket Club dates back to 1875, when cricket was played on a field off Lower Kings Road between the canal and the railway. The land was owned by Lord Brownlow. In 1880 an arrangement was made for the boys of Berkhamsted School, who had previously been playing in the castle grounds, to share the field with the cricket team.

Fact File

Frank Broome

In the 1932-33 season a 17-year-old Berkhamsted lad, Frank Broome, scored 53 goals. In 1934 he turned professional with Aston Villa. No transfer fee was involved, but later Berkhamsted Town received a donation of £25. Frank Broome played regularly in the First Division and in 1946 he transferred to Derby County. He won seven England caps.

BILLET LANE FORD c1890 ZZZ04939
(Berkhamsted Local History and Museum Society)

This is now the main route to Northbridge Way Industrial Estate.

In the 1880s Mr G H Gowring joined the staff of Berkhamsted School. A keen golfer, he formed the Berkhamsted Golf Club in December 1890. He obtained permission to clear sufficient gorse to make a 9-hole golf course - later it was extended to an 18-hole course. In 1923 Edwin Williams of Gorseside purchased 489 acres of Berkhamsted Common for the Golf Club. In the 1930s the club entered into an agreement with the Citizens Association and the Council which granted local people the legal right to enjoy 'air and exercise' on this part of the Common, and this continues to this day.

The town's expansion is also reflected in its shops. The 1791 Directory shows that there were about 50 shopkeepers for a population of 1,350. They are likely to have been in the High Street close to the Market House, in Castle Street, Mill Street, and the adjacent alleys. Most occupied the front rooms of cottages; sometimes a bow window allowed its owners to display wares. Between 1824 and 1839 the number of bakers increased from six to eight, boot makers from eight to twelve, butchers from five to nine, tailors from five to seven, and grocers from ten to 23. In 1890 Berkhamsted shoppers had ten tailors, eleven dressmakers, three laundresses, four watchmakers, seven coal merchants, and 24 boot makers. Milk was delivered three times a day, but milk, cheese, cream and butter could also be bought at dairies or creameries.

The foundation of the Berkhamsted Co-operative Society in 1883 brought a new kind of retailing. Originally provisions were sold to members of the society in the Red Lion (on the site of the HSBC bank). The movement grew rapidly, occupying shops in several parts of the town. As the town had grown during the second half of the century, shops and trades had spread out from the central area, scattered along new streets.

At the time of the 1851 census there were few houses on the southern slopes of the town,

HIGH STREET c1955 B407035

This view looks back towards St Peter's.

apart from some in Kings Road and Chesham Road, and 44 artisans' houses in Highfield Road, known then as Prospect Place. In 1851 the Pilkington Manor estate east of Castle Street was sold; the land was developed in the Manor Street, Ravens Lane and Holliday Street area with small industries, sawmills, artisans' dwellings and principally Cooper's sheep-dip works. In 1868, farmland at Kitsbury had been sold, and streets of middle-class villas were built on the hill south of the High Street. In 1879 land belonging to Boxwell House was sold. From 1888 more streets were built up the hillside between Kings Road and Cross Oak Road on land which had been part of the Kingshill estate. In 1885 Lower Kings Road was built by public subscription to make access easier from the High Street to the station. Nevertheless, Berkhamsted still numbered a mere 5,000 souls at the close of the century.

So much remains of 19th-century Berkhamsted, including many individual buildings in the High Street too numerous to mention, and whole streets of little cottages and larger villas. Walk along the High Street and cast your eyes upwards, and you will see that many houses show the dates of their building. At 173 High Street two fine Victorian chemist's advertisements were recently uncovered. On the other side of the street is Dickman's, another chemist. Go inside and you will see the Victorian wooden drawers with their little labels used to store medicines and powders for making up prescriptions. A little further along is the Victorian window of a baker's shop.

So we leave 19th-century Berkhamsted. The telephone exchange, operating from the front room of a house in Chapel Street, has just arrived, but it was to be many years before it was widely used. Bicycles are seen frequently on the streets, and in 1897 Mr J W Wood, the iron founder, has become the proud owner of a second-hand Benz motor car. However, many years were to pass before cars became a feature of life in the town. Horse-drawn carts were a common sight until well into the 1930s.

TUDOR HOUSE IN BACK LANE (NOW CHURCH LANE) c1890
ZZZ04940 (Berkhamsted Local History and Museum Society)

This house was demolished in 1916 to make room for the Court Theatre, which later became Tesco.

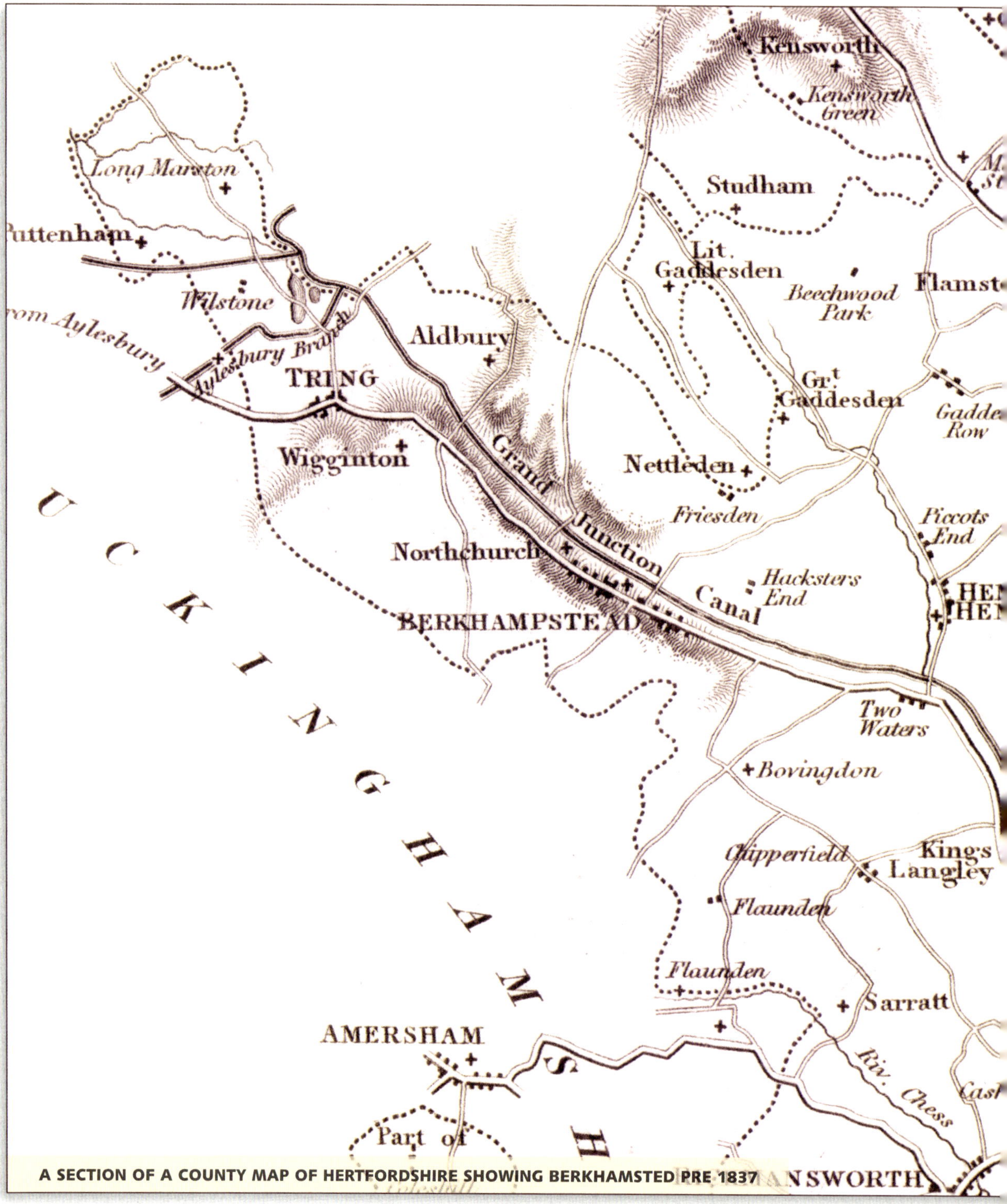

A SECTION OF A COUNTY MAP OF HERTFORDSHIRE SHOWING BERKHAMSTED PRE 1837

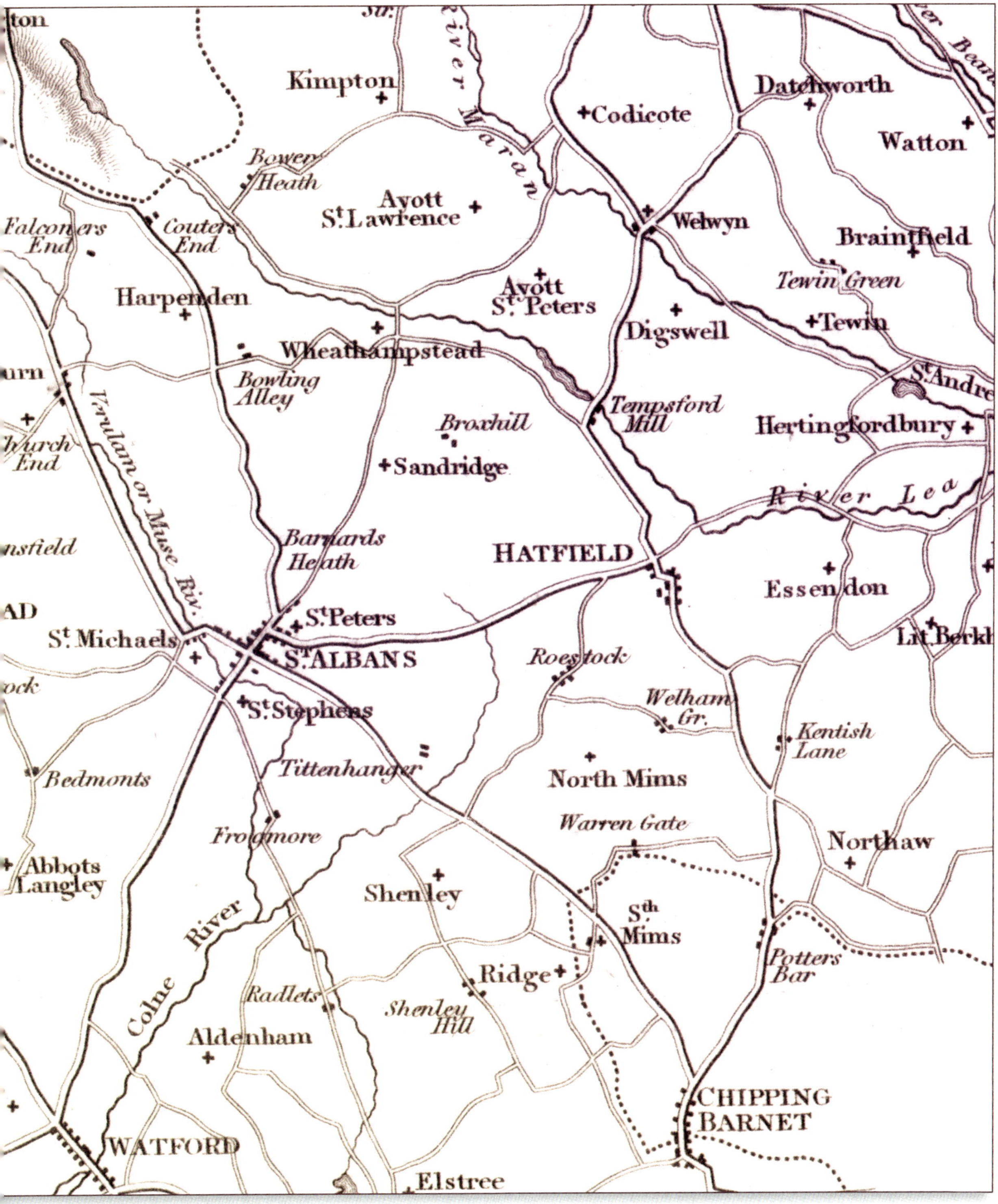
Kimpton
River Maran
Codicote
Datchworth
Watton
Bowers Heath
Avott St. Lawrence
Welwyn
Falconers End
Couters End
Braintfield
Tewin Green
Harpenden
Avott St. Peters
Tewin
Digswell
Wheathampstead
Bowling Alley
St. Andre
Tempsford Mill
Hertingfordbury
Broxhill
Sandridge
Verulam or Muse Riv.
River Lea
Barnards Heath
HATFIELD
Essendon
St. Peters
St. Michaels
St. ALBANS
Lit. Berkh
Roestock
St. Stephens
Welham Gr.
Kentish Lane
Bedmonts
Tittenhanger
North Mims
Warren Gate
Frogmore
Northaw
Abbots Langley
Shenley
Colne River
Sth Mims
Potters Bar
Ridge
Radlets
Shenley Hill
Aldenham
CHIPPING BARNET
WATFORD
Elstree

BARCLAYS
BANK
KINGS ROAD

CHAPTER FOUR

WAR AND GROWTH

GRABALL ROW c1900 ZZZ04941 (Berkhamsted Local History and Museum Society)

The house at the left of the picture is the same as that shown in ZZZ04940 on page 85.

THE FIRST half of the 20th century saw two world wars which were to change the lives of many in Berkhamsted, as elsewhere. Not long after the outbreak of the First World War, men of the Inns of Court Officer Training Corps arrived in the town. In the next few years thousands of these young men, many of whom were later to lose their lives, trained for war in the countryside around Berkhamsted. At the end of September 1914 four infantry companies pitched their tents in Berkhamsted Park, whilst the cavalry set up base in the old Locke & Smith brewery buildings in Water Lane. Two large marquees were erected in the castle grounds for a musketry school. During 1915 the number of men billeted in our little town reached 2,500. Soldiers' church services were a weekly event, and the Rector of St Peter's regularly addressed large congregations.

In Berkhamsted small regimental hospitals were set up at Barncroft and at The Beeches (which was later to become a boarding house for the Girls' Grammar School). Large sheds at Key's timber yard in Castle Street provided mess rooms, whilst the Court House was used as an orderly room. On Armistice Day the bands of the Inns of Court paraded along the High Street and a great bonfire was lit in the Park. Two war memorials record the tragic loss of life: one on the Common shows that 2,000 young men of the Inns of Court did not return, while the other (originally in the High Street close to Tesco, later moved near St Peter's Church) lists the names of 144 local men who perished. A Roll of Honour in Berkhamsted School, now the Collegiate School, lists the 200 old boys who gave their lives in the service of their country.

THE COMMON AT WAR

THE COMMON AND THE FORMER BERKHAMSTED PARK 2005 ZZZ04956 (Ken Wallis)

On 1 August 1916 King George V visited the parade ground in Berkhamsted Park, watched drill practice and bayonet fighting, observed trench fighting and bombing on the Common, and inspected wood fighting in Frithsden beeches. Lord Brownlow had placed his estate at the disposal of the Inns of Court. His waiting room at the station became the Quartermaster's office and stores, and part of Ashridge House became a military hospital. Voluntary Aid Detachments of the local Red Cross helped staff this.

THE INNS OF COURT MEMORIAL, THE COMMON 2005 ZZZ04957 (Ken Wallis)

Fact File

The part of the Park used for exercises by the Inns of Court became known as Kitchener's Field (ZZZ04958, below). On the Common old trenches dug out at this time are still visible. In 1917 the Court Theatre opened in the town to provide films, plays and musicals for the troops. It closed in 1960 and was converted for use by Tesco. Following a fire in 1969, the present supermarket was built.

Before leaving the First World War we should mention one prominent local figure, who could be called 'Britain's Forgotten Hero', General Sir Horace Smith-Dorrien of Haresfoot. Horace was the eleventh child of Robert Algernon Smith, brother of Augustus Smith. He was educated at Harrow and Sandhurst. During the Boer War he was promoted to Major-General. At the start of the First World War he became Commander of the British Second Corps. His finest hour came when the British forces were retreating from Mons. Smith-Dorrien ignored Field Marshal French's orders and made a stand at Le Cateau with the comment: 'Very well, gentlemen, we will fight.' This rear-guard action checked the German advance and saved the British army. After another clash with French he was removed from command. In December 1915 he was appointed to command the forces in German East Africa, but fell ill and was invalided home. General Sir Horace Smith-Dorrien was regarded as a man with a high sense of duty and affection for those who served under him. He has been largely exonerated by the judgement of time.

KITCHENER'S FIELD 2005 ZZZ04958 (Ken Wallis)

THE TOWN HALL AND THE CATTLE MARKET c1920 ZZZ04942 (Berkhamsted Local History and Museum Society)

On the death of Earl Brownlow in 1921 his executors were directed to sell Ashridge to meet death duties. Property developers were immediately interested, for since the war the demand for housing had grown tremendously, and Berkhamsted had good schools and a railway link. On the other hand, the realisation that acres of magnificent trees might be felled and that woodlands which had provided recreation for the people of Berkhamsted for generations might be lost provoked quick reaction.

FRITHSDEN BEECHES, THE ASHRIDGE ESTATE 2005
ZZZ04959 (Ken Wallis)

Already an offer had been made by a syndicate to buy the entire estate. There was no time to be lost. An anonymous offer of £20,000 had been received, which would enable part of the land to be bought for the National Trust. A petition organised locally was sent to the Prime Minister, Stanley Baldwin, appealing for funds. In October 1925 a letter signed by Stanley Baldwin, Ramsay McDonald, Lord Grey of Falloden and Lord Asquith supporting proposals to acquire Ashridge Park for the National Trust appeared in The Times. An appeal for funds was launched, and by the middle of November £40,000 had been raised. 1,700 acres were purchased by the Trust, and in the following year a further 165 acres.

Meanwhile the local MP, Lord Davidson, had been using his influence in high places. In June 1928 it was disclosed that the house and 235 acres had been purchased for the Conservative Party as an educational and political training centre, ensuring the preservation of the mansion and the beautiful gardens, which we still enjoy to this day. Thus the Bonar Law Memorial College came into being, a residential college for the study of social and political science. Its Board of Governors was later widened to include leading representatives of industry.

ASHRIDGE COLLEGE c1965 B407095

In 1959 Ashridge became an independent college devoted to management training. Now Ashridge Management College is known world-wide.

The 1930s saw the demolition of several large houses in the town. At the top of Highfield Road, Highfield House was demolished. The Hall fell victim to dry rot, and the fine building, used in its latter days as the Preparatory Department of Berkhamsted School, was demolished. Most of this estate was developed before the Second World War. Richard Mabey, the naturalist, played cowboys and Indians with his friends in the remaining parkland during the war years, and perhaps acquired his first interest in natural history at that time. After the war, Lombardy Drive and Swing Gate School were built on this site.

Another fine house to fall victim was Egerton House, an Elizabethan house in the High Street. There, in the early years of the century, lived the Llewellyn Davies family, on whose children J M Barrie based 'Peter Pan'. This house was demolished to make way for the Rex Cinema, opened in 1938, designed by the architect David Nye.

In 1921 the number of houses in the Urban District was 1,670, only 23 more than in 1911. In places, as many as eight householders shared one water tap, and many older properties were in a sorry state. Council estates were built in Gossoms End, Swing Gate Lane, Highfield and Northchurch. Following the sale of the Ashridge estate, more private houses were built north of the railway.

Fact File

One of the first performances of 'Peter Pan' took place at Egerton House, staged especially for the Llewellyn Davies children, one of whom was ill. When Egerton House was under threat of demolition, help was sought from James Barrie, but he was too ill to help.

The 1930s saw the arrival of a new building which is very much a feature of our landscape today. In 1928 the London Foundling Hospital had been demolished; the children were housed temporarily in St Anne's School, Redhill, whilst the governors sought an appropriate new site in the country. After considering a number of sites, the Foundling Hospital purchased Ashlyns Hall and a large part of the estate, choosing the site for its healthy location 500 feet above sea level, its proximity to the railway station, and to a town with sufficient amusement for the staff! The nearby playing fields of Berkhamsted School were seen as an added advantage.

John Mortimer Sheppard was selected as architect. Every attempt was made to re-invoke the spirit of the original Foundling Hospital. Much had been saved from that building, and was incorporated in the new one. In June 1933, HRH Prince Arthur of Connaught laid the foundation stone; the children moved to the new buildings in July 1935.

OLD AND NEW AT THE FOUNDLING HOSPITAL

The Foundling Hospital coat of arms was based on the original, designed by William Hogarth.

The staircase which had been in the former girls' wing was installed in the new building. The columns in the band room were an exact copy of the old ones, and the busts of the musicians were reinstated. The original light pedestals were placed along the drive. The statue of Thomas Coram, the founder of the Foundling Hospital in the 18th century, was re-erected on a new base. The old stained glass windows from the London chapel were installed in the new chapel, and the more recent ones in the concert hall; in the balcony, previous seating was re-used. The memorials to governors and secretaries of the Hospital, together with the tomb and remains of Thomas Coram and a bust of Handel, were placed in the crypt. Handel's organ was installed in the chapel.

THE FOUNDLING HOSPITAL, THE OPENING CEREMONY JULY 1935 ZZZ04943
(Berkhamsted Local History and Museum Society)

Prince Arthur of Connaught and other dignitaries meet some of the young girls.

Fact File

When the estate was purchased, the Foundling Hospital was required by the Land Registry to place 20 boundary posts round the estate. These were a copy of the posts in London, with the carving of a lamb. Several still remain today, including one in Hilltop Road and one near Velvet Lawn.

The Foundling Hospital and its children formed an integral part of Berkhamsted life for the next 20 years. At first the governors found no difficulty in meeting costs, but in the post-war years problems were experienced. Following the 1944 Education Act, the Foundling Hospital sought a grant from Hertfordshire County Council for the education of its children in what was now called the Thomas Coram Schools. Additionally, the 1944 Education Act necessitated the reorganisation of the Berkhamsted schools. The two grammar schools became independent. The accommodation at Victoria School was too cramped for the secondary modern school; a new site was sought, the most favoured being one at Greenway.

Meanwhile the situation at the Foundling Hospital was changing. The Hospital now wished to board out the children in foster homes and to arrange for them to attend local schools; thus the numbers requiring residential accommodation was dwindling. In 1951 the Thomas Coram Schools opened as a secondary modern school with the name of Ashlyns School. At the end of the summer term of 1954 the remaining residential children left Berkhamsted. After lengthy negotiations, the sale of the school and most of the Foundling Hospital Estate to Hertfordshire County Council was completed in September 1955. Ashlyns School became a bi-lateral school with both a secondary modern and a grammar section,

ASHLYNS SCHOOL c1955 B407039

and in the 1960s it became a comprehensive school. With the introduction of the three-tier system of education in Berkhamsted in the 1970s, it became the Upper School for 13-19 year olds for the town. It is now a Foundation School under Hertfordshire County Council.

During the Second World War, American and Dutch as well as British troops trained in the area. Food rationing was introduced in January 1940, and the 'Dig for Victory' campaign led to over 1,000 allotments being established in Berkhamsted by May 1941. Many iron railings, including those round St Peter's Church, were removed to make weapons. The Air Raid Precautions Control Centre was established in the Town Hall and manned 24 hours a day. During the war the Town Hall was also used as a British Restaurant, where a hot meal could be obtained for 1s 6d without the use of coupons.

In 1940 the Local Defence Volunteers, later known as the Home Guard, was set up, and observation posts were established throughout the town. The worst period for bombing was September and October 1940, when bombs fell almost daily, mostly on open ground. A house in Shootersway was badly damaged, and the Sunnyside railway bridge was destroyed in the summer of 1941, derailing a train, fortunately without anyone suffering serious injury.

During the war hundreds of London children were evacuated to Berkhamsted. 300 girls from South Hampstead High School shared facilities with the Girls' School. Shelters fitted with bunks were dug in the school grounds. The local schools could not cope with the increase in population, and a shift system came into operation: local children attended school in the morning, and the evacuees attended in the afternoon. Some families with relatives in the town also moved out from London.

FOUNDLING HOSPITAL RELICS

With the sale of the Hospital buildings, the mortal remains of Thomas Coram were removed to St Andrew's Church, Holborn, together with the Handel organ. Plans to reinstate his statue elsewhere failed, and where his statue once stood is a piece of modern art. All the other artefacts from the original Foundling Hospital remain in the school, including the memorials, the stained glass windows, and the staircase. It is a sad fact that problems with flooding in the crypt, first noted in 1961, have become worse in recent years, with the result that the decorated communion rail, some of the memorials, and the bust of Handel have deteriorated. In 2003, at the instigation of Berkhamsted Local History & Museum Society, the buildings were listed Grade II.

Fact File

One of these children was the actor Derek Fowlds, who came with his mother and sister from London to live with his grandmother in Ellesmere Road. He attended Chapel Street Infants' School, Victoria School and Ashlyns School. After his National Service he gave up his apprenticeship with the Clunbury Press to attend RADA.

To escape the risk of London bombing many major statues were evacuated from London to spend the war years among the ruins of Berkhamsted Castle. From the autumn of 1941 to the autumn of 1942 another notable figure took refuge in Berkhamsted, General de Gaulle. During his exile he lived at Rodinghead near Ashridge and attended Mass in the former Roman Catholic church in Park View Road, later to become Marlin Montessori Nursery School.

As in the First World War, Ashridge was requisitioned as a military and civil hospital, but on a much larger scale. Between 1940 and 1946 some 3,000 babies were born at

THE COURT HOUSE, BACK (CHURCH) LANE AND THE WAR MEMORIAL 2005 ZZZ04960 (Ken Wallis)

The war memorial, paid for by public subscription, was erected in 1921 and originally stood in the High Street close to Water Lane. It was moved to its present position in 1952.

Ashridge. To accommodate the many patients, huts were built in the grounds. With the closure of the hospital after the war, these huts were used by the Public Record Office as a repository. It remained there until 1980 when it moved to Kew.

In the months leading up to the D-Day invasion there was a noticeable build-up of troops and equipment around Berkhamsted. In addition to training exercises, convoys of vehicles were kept under cover of the trees at Ashridge and along New Road, Berkhamsted. Field Marshal Montgomery and General Eisenhower visited to inspect the progress and supervise the preparations. With the end of the war in May 1945, Berkhamsted celebrated with street parties. The chairman of the Urban District Council quoted from the telegram sent to Winston Churchill: 'Together we pray that we build a better Britain and a better Berkhamsted.'

The need for housing was even greater after the Second World War than after the First. Before more housing could begin, prefabs were set up in Three Close Lane. Soon after, a further 200 council houses were built on the Durrants Estate and later on the Westfield Estate, and in the 1960s and 70s on the Ashlyns Estate. During the early 1960s the upper reaches of Bridgewater Road and South Park Gardens were developed, and, with the demolition of Berkhamsted Place in 1967, also the roads higher up the hillside. Still further expansion came in the 1970s

LOWER KINGS ROAD c1955 B407006

Still a busy junction today, Lower Kings Road was built in 1885 by public subscription to make a more direct route to the new railway station. The long tradition of a greengrocer's shop on the corner has now been broken.

and 1980s with the building of the Chiltern Park Estate on Tunnel Hill Fields - it was here on the lower slopes that the people of Berkhamsted once watched the circus. In the last decades of the century there was much infilling in the grounds of large houses and the building of flats on brown-field sites, where garages or industry once were. The growth of the town was given a further impetus with the electrification of the railway in 1965.

Even in a ruined state, the castle remained a focal point for the people of Berkhamsted. In June 1864 the Duke of Cornwall had granted Earl Brownlow 'the Site and Remains of Berkhampstead Castle ... at £1 per annum ... Lord Brownlow has no actual benefit from the property, he merely maintains it for the recreation of the inhabitants of Berkhampstead.' We have read of the castle as a favourite spot for courting couples, as a training ground for musketry, and as a refuge for the London statues during the war, but it has witnessed much more besides.

An unusual event was the landing in the castle grounds in 1913 of the Army dirigible (airship) 'Gamma', captained by J N Fletcher, an old boy of Berkhamsted School. In June 1935, after visiting both the Girls' School and the Boys' School, the Prince of Wales, later Edward VIII, visited the castle, where he met a large assembled gathering of ex-servicemen, Girl Guides and Boy Scouts, children from the elementary schools, and other representatives of the community. He was the first Duke of Cornwall to pay an official visit to the Manor of Berkhamsted since 1616.

The castle grounds witnessed several historical pageants; the first was in 1922, 700 years after the building of St Peter's Church. This was written by the eminent historian G M Trevelyan, who lived in the town. He played the part of Chaucer. The same pageant was repeated in 1931. The 900th anniversary of the submission of the English to William the Conqueror was celebrated in 1966 with a large pageant. Those who are too young to remember these pageants will have fond memories of the many Bank Holiday fetes held annually, until very recently, in the castle grounds. Unfortunately, concerns about damage from marquees, and health and safety regulations, have meant that annual fêtes no longer take place in the castle grounds, but on Kitchener's Field instead.

THE CASTLE c1955 B407025

THE PAINTED CHAMBER AND THE CHAPEL, BERKHAMSTED CASTLE 2005 ZZZ04961 (Ken Wallis)

The first cinema in Berkhamsted was the Gem, a corrugated iron hut in Cowper Road, specially adapted in 1910. Before this films had been shown in the Town Hall, and by a travelling show in the meadow by the Crooked Billet. The Gem did not survive competition from the Picture Playhouse, which opened in 1912 in Prince Edward Street. With the opening of the Court Theatre in 1917 the Playhouse closed, and its cinema seats were transferred to the Court. The building was renamed the Kings Hall and continued in use until the 1980s, when it was replaced by an office block, Fells House. The Court Theatre originally had a dome, which was removed in 1934. The Court was somewhat eclipsed by the opening of the new Rex in 1938, but it retained its facilities, and the Berkhamsted Amateur Operatic and Dramatic Society staged many productions there. In 1960 the theatre was sold and became a Tesco store.

In 1976 the Rex was converted: the circle became two cinemas, while the stalls went over to full-time bingo. In February 1988 the building closed at the expiry of the lease. News that the building had been sold to a property developer reached the Cinema Theatre Association, who managed to have it spot listed Grade II two days before it closed. The new owners immediately applied for permission to demolish the building and develop the site. The people of Berkhamsted responded with a campaign to save the Rex as an arts centre and a cinema. Throughout the 1990s negotiations and campaigning continued.

Eventually the property developers, Nicholas King Homes, secured permission to build a complex of flats next to the cinema. The auditorium was leased to James Hannaway, and after several postponements the Rex cinema opened once more in December 2004 as a one-screen cinema. The interior has been beautifully renovated. It is rather sad that cinemagoers no longer approach through the foyer, but by means of steps at the side - the foyer is now a restaurant. But the Rex is open once more!

Fact File

After the Court Theatre was sold in 1960, the Operatic and Dramatic Society performed in the Kings Hall and the Civic Centre. In 1970 the Society staged 'A Day in the Death of Joe Egg', with nine-year old Sarah Brightman playing the part of Joe as a child. Sarah's mother was an active member of the society for many years; her father built a number of houses in the town in the 1970s and 1980s. Sarah Brightman has since gone on to West End success, notably in 'The Phantom of the Opera'.

THE CANAL AND LOCK c1965 B407108

We are at Lower Kings Road. Through the trees we can see Castle Mill, built in 1910 and used for the manufacture of animal feeding stuffs by J G Knowles & Son; it had a small wharf for canal boats. It ceased operating after the Second World War. Used as offices for some years, it is now being converted into housing.

Earlier in the century another important building was very nearly lost, but it was saved by the people of Berkhamsted, who had contributed towards its establishment in the first place. In the 1960s it was clear that the Town Hall was in need of adaptation to meet new fire regulations. The building was closed, and in the 1970s it became derelict and the victim of vandalism. It was the subject of a dispute which lasted for six and a half years. Berkhamsted Town Council, the corporate trustee, was advised that the building was beyond repair. It was decided to build a new hall behind the High Street façade, but this plan was frustrated, first because of a defect in the title, and subsequently by a moratorium on local government capital expenditure. The council tried to sell the building, but permission was refused by the Charity Commission because of local opposition led by the Rescue and Action Group, which included among its number three sixteen-year-old boys from Ashlyns School. The group was supported by well-known Berkhamsted personalities: Graham Greene and Sir Hugh Carleton Greene (whose father Charles Henry Greene was Headmaster of Berkhamsted School), Richard Mabey, and Antony Hopkins, the musician and composer.

The Rescue and Action Group won the day. In 1979 a new Town Hall Trust was established, which succeeded in restoring the Town Hall to full use during the period between 1982 and 1999. Some modification was made to the original design, the most notable being the alteration to the main staircase. In 1983 the Trust converted the ground floor into a shopping arcade called Lamb's Shops, which was formally opened by Lord Bernard Miles on 31 December 1983. Trade flourished throughout the 1980s, but changing patterns of retail trading led to the Trust entering into a 25-year lease with City Centre Restaurants, which converted most of the ground floor into a Caffé Uno.

In 1999 further restoration work took place with the help of a substantial Heritage Lottery Fund grant and public support. The former Institute Room was restored and reopened under the name of the Clock Room. The Town Hall is now a popular building with three rooms for hire for varying functions. At the rear of the building on the ground floor is a craft centre, The

THE TOWN HALL 2005 ZZZ04962 (Ken Wallis)

Making Place. Further restoration work is planned, when funds allow.

The early 1970s saw the reorganisation of the state schools in Berkhamsted with the establishment of the three-tier system of first and middle schools and Ashlyns School as the Upper School. With the exception of the Roman Catholic Primary School, all the primary schools became first schools. The first middle school to be established was Augustus Smith Middle School, near Velvet Lawn; the second was Thomas Bourne Church of England Middle School at the top of Durrants Lane; and the last to be opened was Bridgewater School, the only school on the north side of town. Park View School, the original British School, then closed. The names of the first two middle schools commemorated two local educational philanthropists. A drop in numbers during the1980s led to the closure of Thomas Bourne Middle School, whose premises were bought by Egerton-Rothesay School and used for its senior department.

The children from Thomas Bourne School transferred to Augustus Smith Middle

Fact File

Egerton-Rothesay School was formed by the merger of two private schools: Rothesay School, founded in the High Street in 1922, later in Shrublands Road, and Egerton School, founded in 1950 in Charles Street. The two schools merged in 1984 and opened a senior department when the Thomas Bourne building became vacant. The new department was opened by the Prime Minister, Margaret Thatcher, in September 1988.

ASHLYNS SCHOOL c1955 B407042

This is the main entrance.

School, and that school was renamed Thomas Coram. It is ironic that 40 years previously the Urban and County Councils had resisted the retention of the name Thomas Coram because of its association with foundlings, and the name Ashlyns had been chosen instead.

For a number of years it had been suggested that Berkhamsted School and Berkhamsted Girls' School should join together, to the benefit of the children from both schools. This had been resisted, especially by Girls' School parents. In 1996 the two schools came together with the name of Berkhamsted Collegiate School, and Dr Priscilla Chadwick was appointed as first principal. Older residents still refer to the Castle Street and Kings Road campuses as the Boys' and Girls' Schools.

For the greater part of the century the affairs of Berkhamsted had been governed by the Berkhamsted Urban District Council and the Berkhamsted Rural District Council; the former was based in the Civic Centre, opened in 1938, and the latter in Boxwell House. With the local government reorganisation in 1974 these bodies were dissolved, and Berkhamsted became part of Dacorum Council, based in Hemel Hempstead. At first Berkhamsted was left with only a parish council, but in 1976 this became a town council with the right to elect a mayor. This government from Hemel Hempstead has been resented by many in Berkhamsted, which jealously guards its identity, and many of the ills of the latter years have been placed, rightly or wrongly, at the doors of Dacorum Borough Council.

BERKHAMSTED SCHOOL c1960 B407055

Between the library and the chapel, the cloisters lead through to Deans' Hall.

This independent spirit was further shown when a group of local citizens, feeling that the existing Town Council did not represent the wishes of the people of Berkhamsted, swept to victory in the 1995 elections under the banner of 'Berkhamsted First', taking the majority of the fifteen seats. Lack of experience meant that their control of the council was short-lived, but it was a rude awakening for several long-standing councillors.

Fact File

The people of Berkhamsted have never forgiven Dacorum Borough Council for filling in the town's open-air swimming pool, built in 1923. Many a Berkhamsted child first learned to swim in the chilly waters of that pool. The town now has a large sports centre with an indoor pool, but people still speak nostalgically of the old swimming pool.

THE GRAND UNION CANAL c1960 B407049

The Canal and Riverside Partnership have now made the towpath easier for mothers with pushchairs and older members of the community. Shaw & Kilburn's Garage, now replaced by Greenes Court, can be seen through the trees.

As early as 1927 the need for a bypass was first mooted, but it was not until 1993 that the A41 bypass was finally completed. Delays were caused by disputes over the route. On completion of the bypass, traffic-calming measures were introduced in the town centre.

We have already referred to sports activities and operatic and dramatic societies, but Berkhamsted has much more to offer. The first meeting of the Berkhamsted Citizens Association was held in the castle grounds in 1924, 'its sole aim being to represent the interests of the citizen'. Over the years it has provided a forum for the airing of local concerns on many issues. In 1929 the Berkhamsted Art Society was formed, and has remained active ever since. In the field of music the Berkhamsted Choral Society, originally the Wayfarers' Choral Society, has been active since 1930. The Music Society, with Antony Hopkins as president, has been flourishing since 1954.

Concern that little was being done to preserve our historical heritage led to the formation in 1950 of the Berkhamsted & District Local History Society, now the Berkhamsted Local History & Museum Society. The society holds an exhibition every three years and has a growing collection of artefacts, now housed in the Dacorum

SUNNYSIDE ALLOTMENTS 2005 ZZZ04963 (Ken Wallis)

Members of a local art class appreciate the flowers.

Heritage Trust's Museum Store behind the Civic Centre. An off-shoot of this society is the Berkhamsted and District Archaeological Society, formed in 1972. We must not forget the Cowper Society, the Jazz Society, the Film Society, the Geography Society, the Chess Club and many more. In 1997 the Graham Greene Birthplace Trust was established and holds a four-day festival annually, which draws people from all over the world. The activities of most of the art and cultural societies are co-ordinated by the Berkhamsted Arts Trust, supported by Dacorum Borough Council, which provides deficit guarantees to societies.

Many well-known literary and broadcasting figures associated with the town have already received passing mention; others include W W Jacobs, the noted short story writer, who lived in Chesham Road, and H E Todd, who lived in Brownlow Road, and in his retirement wrote the Bobby Brewster stories for children. Among those born in the town were Peter Quennell, the writer, whose parents are known for their book 'A History of Everyday Things in England', and the religious writer and broadcaster Gerald Priestland. His uncle was Sir Richard Ashmole Cooper of the local firm Messrs William Cooper & Nephews, which became Cooper, McDougall & Robertson in 1925.

Since it was formed in the 1840s, this firm had

DEAN INCENT'S HOUSE 2005 ZZZ04964 (Ken Wallis)

The sign was painted by David Sherratt c1990. This house features on Berkhamsted's Heritage Walk, established for the millennium.

A COOPER ADVERTISEMENT c1910 ZZZ04916 ê
(Berkhamsted Local History and Museum Society)

Over the years Coopers produced many colourful and amusing posters advertising their range of products.

expanded worldwide and diversified to meet the needs of the 20th century. From 1937 the company worked with ICI to produce horticultural products under the trade name of Plant Protection. Since 1929, Coopers had been operating a programme of quality stockbreeding at Home Farm, Little Gaddesden, and in 1940 they built a new Technical Bureau in the High Street. Shenstone Court was converted for use as Berkhamsted Hill Research Station, and in 1952 the laboratory facilities at Home Farm moved here. The printing department, Clunbury Press, began to take on commercial work. Synthetic insecticides were produced as aerosols, the first in the country, with brand names such as Cooper's Fly Killer. In 1959 the business was acquired by the Wellcome Foundation. Clunbury Press closed in 1979, and the Research Station was sold in the 1980s to an American pharmaceutical company with animal health interests. In 1992 the business in the town was sold to a French company, Roussel Uclaf, and in 1995 to Agr-Evo UK. It finally closed in 1997, and the site has since been redeveloped as housing.

MANOR STREET 2005 ZZZ04965 (Ken Wallis)

We are looking down towards Chapel Street. The housing on the right replaces part of Cooper's works in this Conservation Area.

The last years of the 19th and the early decades of the 20th century saw the arrival of branches of London banks, together with branches of national stores such as Sainsbury's, Woolworth's, Kinghams, Home & Colonial, W H Smith, Boots, Freeman, Hardy & Willis and Sketchleys. All these shops, with the exception of W H Smith and Boots, have left the town. From the end of the 19th century shops had spread further from the town centre to serve new areas of housing. In the last decades of the 20th century most of these corner shops and sub-post offices have reverted to housing. In recent years an increasing number of Berkhamsted's inhabitants, now numbering some 20,000, commute to London and elsewhere to earn their living.

Many of the local shops and traders listed in the 1937 Kelly's Directory remained until the 1980s. In Lower Kings Road is Saltmarsh, originally in Prince Edward Street, and Baileys, formerly in Castle Street. Kempster is still at the east end of the High Street. With

THE CANAL 2005 ZZZ04966 (Ken Wallis)

This view looks down towards the Crystal Palace from Ravens Lane Lock. Compare this picture with the earlier one of the same scene on page 81. An interpretation desk can be seen to the right of the picture.

the retirement of Alan Dickman in 2003 another family business closed, although the name remains, as does that of Wood's. The number of businesses that have closed is endless: Lane's, Fox's, Lintott's, Leatherdale's, Sanderson's, and White's, to name but a few. Corby, Palmer & Stewart, the Bulbourne clothing mantle factory, the second largest employer in the town in the 1960s, has long since closed its doors, to be replaced by the Lower Kings Road car park. Only street and housing names indicate where Cooper's once was. The removal firm of S Dell & Sons has now moved to premises in Northbridge Road. There are no industries remaining in the town centre. All are now in Northbridge Road or the River Park Industrial Estate.

Food shopping is now virtually restricted to two supermarkets, Waitrose and Tesco Metro, although the recent return of a small Co-op provides an alternative. Public houses are fewer, but pavement cafés, pizza bars and restaurants abound. Building societies, estate agents and charity shops pepper the High Street. One searches in vain in the High Street for material to make dresses or even wool to darn socks.

THE CANAL 2005 ZZZ04967 (Ken Wallis)

CHAPTER FIVE

THE INDEPENDENT SPIRIT LIVES ON

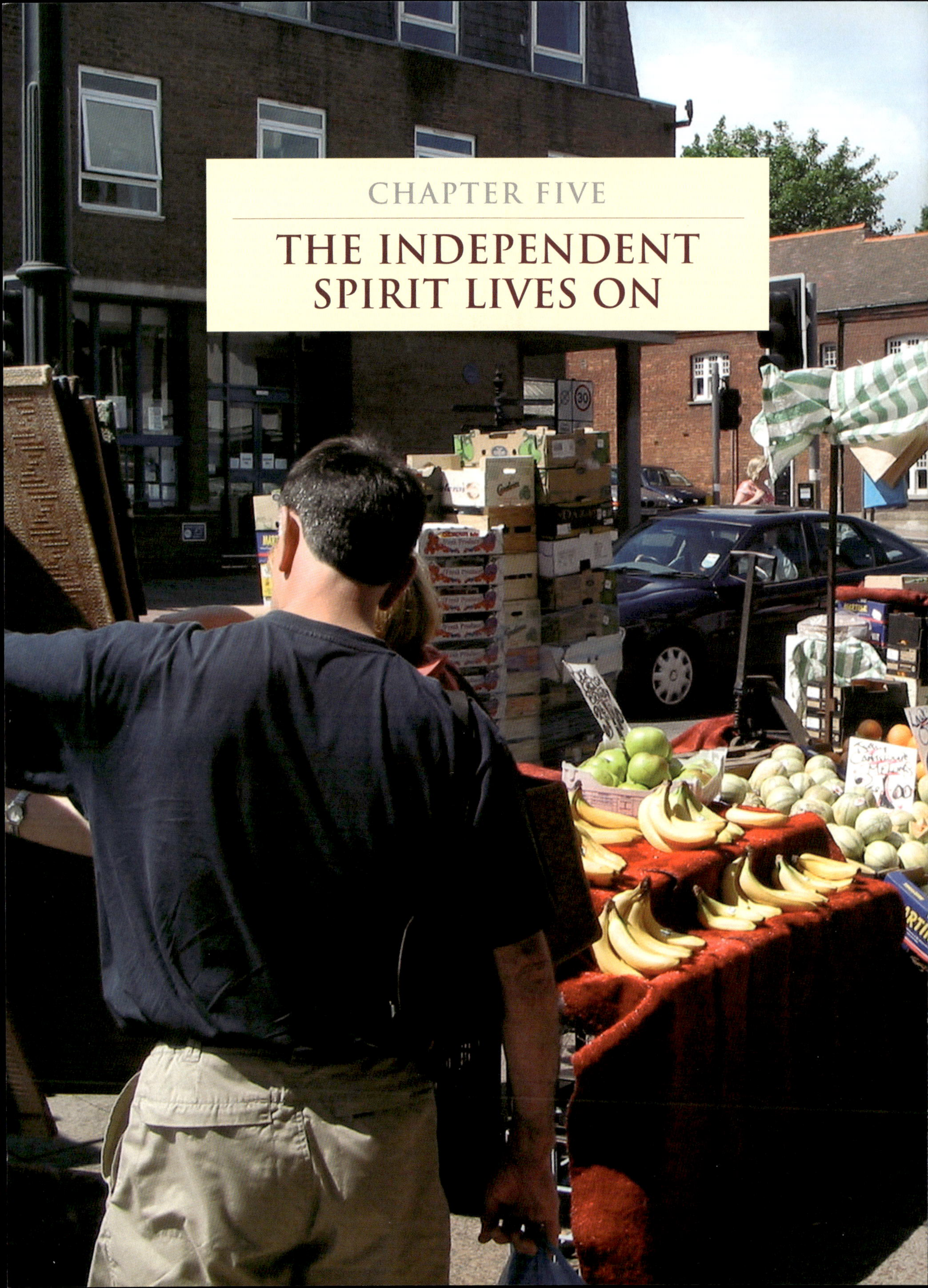

IT IS TIME to leave the ancient town of Berkhamsted, with its rich historical heritage and beautiful surrounding countryside, both of which make it an attractive and pleasant place in which to live. But while capitalising on its past, Berkhamsted does not live in the past. Its people are proud of the place in which they live, and both young and old contribute to its vibrant community.

Walk along the High Street and enjoy the buildings of the different periods, and watch the customers of the pavement cafés chatting together. If it is the third Sunday in the month, the stalls of the Farmers' Market will be spread along the north side of the High Street. Twice a year you will hear a smattering of French from the stallholders of the French Market, which stretches almost from St Peter's Church to beyond the old Bourne School. Surrounding shops are open, making the most of the opportunity for extra trade. How different from the Sundays of yesteryear! Once a month the Saturday Community Market takes place in the Town Hall, whilst the weekly market continues outside, as it has done for many centuries.

At the end of each school day the High Street suddenly becomes crowded, as children pour into the town centre from all directions: down Swing Gate Lane from Thomas Coram School, down Chesham Road from Ashlyns School, and down through Butts Meadow and along Prince Edward Street mud-bespattered Collegiate boys, returning from their sports field, mingle with the children leaving Victoria School with their parents, whilst other Collegiate boys and girls join them from Mill Street and Kings Road.

THE SATURDAY MARKET 2005 ZZZ04968 (Ken Wallis)

THE TOWN HALL AND THE MARKET 2005
ZZZ04969 (Ken Wallis)

One evening every December as darkness falls the High Street is closed to traffic. Christmas lights are switched on, and crowds enjoy the stalls and entertainment of the Festival of Light, close to where the Old Market House once stood.

Almost every evening societies are meeting, either in the Civic Centre or across the road in the Town Hall. Perhaps there is an art or history exhibition, or Oxfam has a sale of children's clothes. Maybe the

Berkhamsted Youth Theatre is staging a play. Auditions for the next Sergeant Pepper Concert are advertised, and the youth of the town will take this opportunity to show their talents in this grand money-raising event, which takes place every summer in the Centenary Hall of the Collegiate School. Not far from this grand hall a new building has just been opened, the Knox-Johnston Sports Centre, commemorating yet another famous old boy.

In Shootersway, planning permission has been granted to the St Francis Hospice to erect a larger building to cater for the terminally ill of Berkhamsted and the surrounding district.

Maybe a film at the Rex takes your fancy, so make your way there passing the Swan Centre, formerly the Swan Inn, where the Youth Council is meeting, or an invited band is playing to a large audience. If it is the beginning of October you will meet visitors from far and wide who are here for the Graham Greene Festival, celebrating the writer's birth, on 2 October 1904 at St John's, Chesham Road.

If you have time to spare, go into St Peter's Church. Enjoy its beauty and serenity, and read the monuments to the many who helped to make the town what it is today. On leaving the church, make your way down Castle Street past the Collegiate School to the canal. Here you can walk in either direction along the towpath and learn more of the history of Berkhamsted from the stone interpretation desks. In May 2003 the Canal and Riverside Partnership (CARP) won the East of England Market Towns Award for Heritage for its work in making the whole canal area into an attractive feature. Where once there were wharves, bustling with activity, you will see canal-side housing; where once working barges chugged their way towards London or Birmingham, you can now watch families enjoying boating holidays.

Return to Castle Street, and make your way to the Castle. Climb the motte to the keep, and survey the town from the ancient defences. Walk around the vast bailey and think of all those who have lived, sought refuge or

The Boote, in Castle Street, is one of several former inns and taverns now no longer licensed.

gathered for celebrations within these walls. The castle, still part of the Duchy of Cornwall, is an unmanned English Heritage site. Negotiations are currently under way between English Heritage, Berkhamsted Town Council and representatives of local societies to make visits to the castle a more worthwhile experience for locals and tourists alike.

Perhaps the green of the surrounding hills tempts you to go further afield. Put on your walking boots - it may be muddy - and make your way up through Kitchener's Field to the Common and perhaps as far as Ashridge. If you are lucky, you may disturb fallow deer in groups of two or three; you may also see isolated muntjac deer, and hear their eerie barking, especially in the early evening.

In this short history and celebration of the town we have tried to give you a taste of Berkhamsted, of how it has developed and how its people have made it what it is today. We hope you have enjoyed it, and that it will encourage you to look more closely at the town in which you live. If you are an outsider, perhaps it will even tempt you to come and live here!

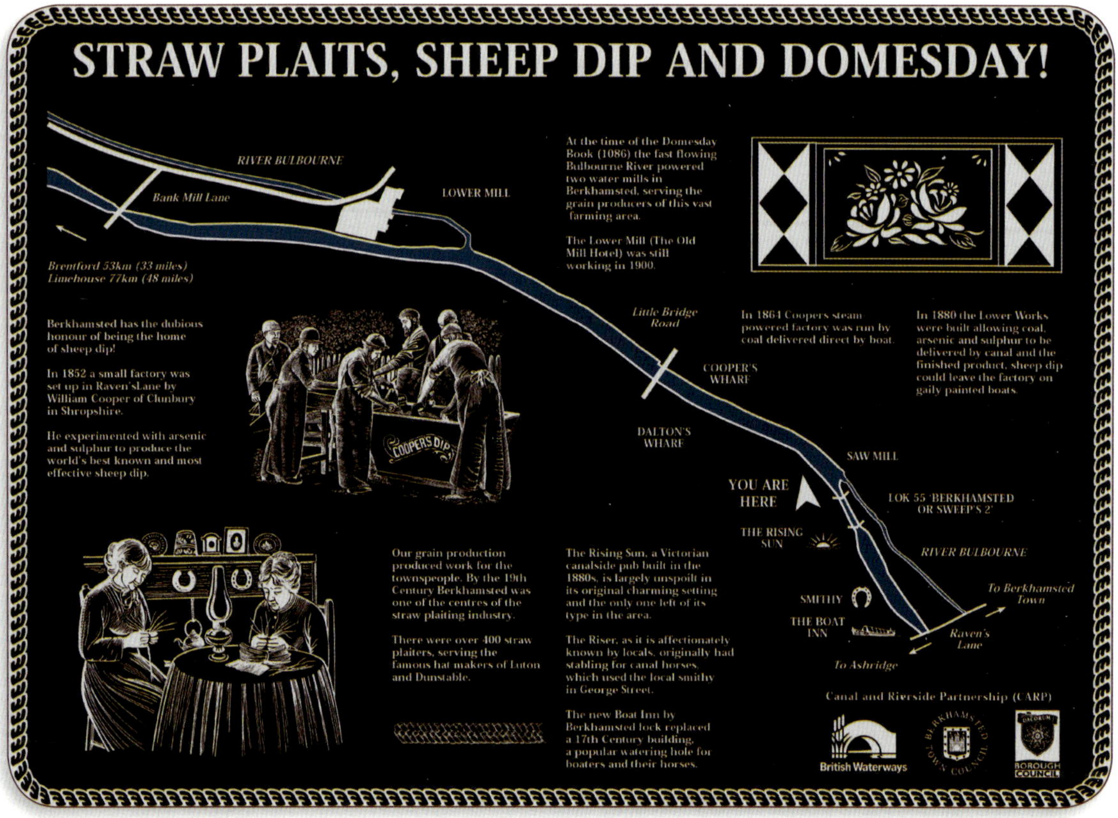

STRAW PLAITS, SHEEP DIP AND DOMESDAY! A CANAL-SIDE INTERPRETATION DESK ZZZ05007 (CARP)

ACKNOWLEDGEMENTS AND BIBLIOGRAPHY

ACKNOWLEDGEMENTS

In preparing this book the Berkhamsted Local History & Museum Society acknowledges the debt owed to its founder members, especially to the notable local historian Percy Birtchnell, and to all those who have in the last 55 years carried out research and helped to gather the extensive collection of old photographs and archives, or who have themselves recorded through photographs the history of our town. We are grateful for the support and assistance of Catherine Peet, the Curator of Dacorum Heritage Trust, to Jan Messent for permission to reproduce the last panels of the Bayeux Tapestry and to Lindy Foster-Weinreb of CARP for permission to reproduce the canal side interpretation desk.

BIBLIOGRAPHY

A Short History of Berkhamsted - Percy C Birtchnell
Berkhamsted, An Illustrated History - Scott Hastie
Reminiscences of Berkhamsted - Henry Nash
History and Antiquities of Berkhamsted - The Rev J Cobb
Berkhamsted St Peter - R A Norris
The History of Berkhamsted Common - George H Whybrow
A History of Berkhamsted School - B H Garnons Williams
The Parks and Gardens of West Hertfordshire - The Hertfordshire Gardens Trust and Tom Williamson
Famous Authors in Hertfordshire - Rudolph Robert
A Prospect of Ashridge - Douglas Coult

Francis Frith

Pioneer Victorian Photographer

Francis Frith, founder of the world-famous photographic archive, was a complex and multi-talented man. A devout Quaker and a highly successful Victorian businessman, he was philosophical by nature and pioneering in outlook. By 1855 he had already established a wholesale grocery business in Liverpool, and sold it for the astonishing sum of £200,000, which is the equivalent today of over £15,000,000. Now in his thirties, and captivated by the new science of photography, Frith set out on a series of pioneering journeys up the Nile and to the Near East.

He was the first photographer to venture beyond the sixth cataract of the Nile. Africa was still the mysterious 'Dark Continent', and Stanley and Livingstone's historic meeting was a decade into the future. The conditions for picture taking confound belief. He laboured for hours in his wicker dark-room in the sweltering heat of the desert, while the volatile chemicals fizzed dangerously in their trays. Back in London he exhibited his photographs and was 'rapturously cheered' by members of the Royal Society. His reputation as a photographer was made overnight.

By the 1870s the railways had threaded their way across the country, and Bank Holidays and half-day Saturdays had been made obligatory by Act of Parliament. All of a sudden the working man and his family were able to enjoy days out, take holidays, and see a little more of the world.

With typical business acumen, Francis Frith foresaw that these new tourists would enjoy having souvenirs to commemorate their days out. For the next thirty years he travelled the country by train and by pony and trap, producing fine photographs of seaside resorts and beauty spots that were keenly bought by millions of Victorians. These prints were painstakingly pasted into family albums and pored over during the dark nights of winter, rekindling precious memories of summer excursions. Frith's studio was soon supplying retail shops all over the country, and by 1890 F Frith & Co had become the greatest specialist photographic publishing company in the world, with over 2,000 sales outlets, and pioneered the picture postcard.

Francis Frith had died in 1898 at his villa in Cannes, his great project still growing. By 1970 the archive he created contained over a third of a million pictures showing 7,000 British towns and villages.

Frith's legacy to us today is of immense significance and value, for the magnificent archive of evocative photographs he created provides a unique record of change in the cities, towns and villages throughout Britain over a century and more. Frith and his fellow studio photographers revisited locations many times down the years to update their views, compiling for us an enthralling and colourful pageant of British life and character.

We are fortunate that Frith was dedicated to recording the minutiae of everyday life. For it is this sheer wealth of visual data, the painstaking chronicle of changes in dress, transport, street layouts, buildings, housing and landscape that captivates us so much today, offering us a powerful link with the past and with the lives of our ancestors.

Computers have now made it possible for Frith's many thousands of images to be accessed almost instantly. The archive offers every one of us an opportunity to examine the places where we and our families have lived and worked down the years. Its images, depicting our shared past, are now bringing pleasure and enlightenment to millions around the world a century and more after his death. For further information visit: www.francisfrith.co.uk

FREE PRINT OF YOUR CHOICE

Mounted Print
Overall size 14 x 11 inches (355 x 280mm)

Choose any Frith photograph in this book. Please note: photographs with a reference number starting with a "Z" are not Frith photographs and cannot be supplied under this offer.
Simply complete the Voucher opposite and return it with your remittance for £2.25 (to cover postage and handling) and we will print the photograph of your choice in SEPIA (size 11 x 8 inches) and supply it in a cream mount with a burgundy rule line (overall size 14 x 11 inches).

Offer valid for delivery to one UK address only.

***PLUS:* Order additional Mounted Prints at HALF PRICE - £7.49 each** (normally £14.99)
If you would like to order more Frith prints from this book, possibly as gifts for friends and family, you can buy them at half price (with no additional postage and handling costs).

***PLUS:* Have your Mounted Prints framed**
For an extra £14.95 per print you can have your mounted print(s) framed in an elegant polished wood and gilt moulding, overall size 16 x 13 inches (no additional postage and handling required).

IMPORTANT!

These special prices are only available if you use this form to order. You must use the ORIGINAL VOUCHER on this page (no copies permitted). We can only despatch to one UK address. This offer cannot be combined with any other offer.

Send completed Voucher form to:
The Francis Frith Collection, Frith's Barn, Teffont, Salisbury, Wiltshire SP3 5QP

CHOOSE A PHOTOGRAPH FROM THIS BOOK

Voucher *for FREE and Reduced Price Frith Prints*

Please do not photocopy this voucher. Only the original is valid, so please fill it in, cut it out and return it to us with your order.

Picture ref no	Page no	Qty	Mounted @ £7.49	Framed + £14.95	Total Cost £
		1	Free of charge*	£	£
			£7.49	£	£
			£7.49	£	£
			£7.49	£	£
			£7.49	£	£
			£7.49	£	£
			* Post & handling		£2.25
			Total Order Cost		£

Please allow 28 days for delivery.
Offer available to one UK address only

Title of this book ....
I enclose a cheque/postal order for £ ....
made payable to 'The Francis Frith Collection'

OR please debit my Mastercard / Visa / Maestro card, details below

Card Number

Issue No (Maestro only) Valid from (Maestro)

Expires Signature

Name Mr/Mrs/Ms ....
Address ....
....
....
.... Postcode ....
Daytime Tel No ....
Email ....

ISBN: 1-84589-195-3 Valid to 31/12/08

FREE PRINT - SEE OVERLEAF

CAN YOU HELP US WITH INFORMATION ABOUT ANY OF THE FRITH PHOTOGRAPHS IN THIS BOOK?

We are gradually compiling an historical record for each of the photographs in the Frith archive. It is always fascinating to find out the names of the people shown in the pictures, as well as insights into the shops, buildings and other features depicted.

If you recognize anyone in the photographs in this book, or if you have information not already included in the author's caption, do let us know. We would love to hear from you, and will try to publish it in future books or articles.

OUR PRODUCTION TEAM

Frith books are produced by a small dedicated team at offices in the converted Grade II listed 18th-century barn at Teffont near Salisbury, illustrated above. Most have worked with the Frith Collection for many years. All have in common one quality: they have a passion for the Frith Collection. The team is constantly expanding, but currently includes:

Paul Baron, Jason Buck, John Buck, Heather Crisp, David Davies, Louis du Mont, Isobel Hall, Lucy Hart, Julian Hight, Peter Horne, James Kinnear, Karen Kinnear, Tina Leary, Stuart Login, Sue Molloy, Miles Murray, Sarah Roberts, Kate Rotondetto, Dean Scource, Eliza Sackett, Terence Sackett, Sandra Sampson, Adrian Sanders, Sandra Sanger, Julia Skinner, Lewis Taylor, Shelley Tolcher, Lorraine Tuck, Miranda Tunnicliffe, David Turner and Ricky Williams.